Exodus to Humanism

EXODUS TO HUMANISM

Jewish Identity Without Religion

David Ibry

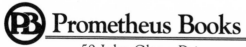 **Prometheus Books**

59 John Glenn Drive
Amherst, New York 14228-2197

Published 1999 by Prometheus Books

03 02 01 00 99   5 4 3 2 1

Library of Congress Cataloging-in-Publication Data

Ibry, David.
     Exodus to humanism : Jewish identity without religion / by David Ibry.
        p.   cm.
     Includes bibliographical references.
     ISBN 1–57392–267–6 (alk. paper)
     1. Humanistic Judaism. 2. Jews—Identity. I. Title.
BM538.H87127   1999
211′.6—dc21   98–47554
                                                                        CIP

Printed in the United States of America on acid-free paper

To honor the memory of my father, Benjamin Ibry,
and my mother, Giulietta dei Crusinallo.

Contents

List of Contributors

(*) means mentioned in *Who's Who Reference*

Prof. Sir Isaiah Berlin (*)	(Introduction)
Prof. Sir Hermann Bondi (*)	(Introduction, chapters 3, 4, 5, 7)
Mr. Geoffrey Elkan	(Chapters 2, 3, 4, 7, 9)
Prof. Albert Ellis (*)	(Chapters 3, 7)
Mr. Sidney Epton	(Chapters 4, 7)
Mrs. Olga Faroqui	(Introduction)
Mr. Michael Goldman	(Chapter 9)
Mr. Howard Gross	(Introduction)
Prof. Adolf Grünbaum (*)	(Chapters 2, 3, 7)
Mrs. Rose Hacker (*)	(Chapter 5)
Mrs. Wendy Hillary	(Chapter 5)
Dr. Harold Hillman	(Chapters 3, 7, 9)
Mrs. Pearl Joseph	(Chapter 4)
Prof. George Klein (*)	(Chapter 2)
Mr. Josh Kutchinsky	(Introduction, chapter 8)
Dr. Henry Morgentaler (*)	(Chapters 5, 9)
Prof. Jean-Claude Pecker (*)	(Introduction, chapters 3, 4, 7)
Prof. Ernest Poser (*)	(Chapters 3, 6)
Prof. Howard Radest (*)	(Chapters 3, 8)

Mrs. Claire Rayner (*)	(Chapters 2, 5)
Dr. Ben Roston (*)	(Chapter 8)
Prof. Evry Schatzman (*)	(Introduction, chapter 7)
Mr. Leonard Sterling	(Chapters 4, 9)
Mrs. Helen Suzman (*)	(Chapter 2)
Mr. Arnold Wesker (*)	(Chapter 9)
Mr. Derek Wilkes	(Introduction, chapters 5, 6)

Acknowledgments

The writing, the compilation, the editing, and the correspondence with the twenty-seven contributors of this book have occupied me for more time than I care to contemplate and over the course of this time I have accumulated a number of debts. Of these perhaps the most outstanding are the debts for the support and encouragement I received from Prof. Sir Hermann Bondi, Mr. Geoffrey Elkan, Dr. Harold Hillman, and my publisher, Prometheus Books.

I entered the Lager as a non-believer, and as a non-believer I was liberated and have lived to this day.

Primo Levi
The Drowned and the Saved

Preface

This book provides an answer to the question: Is religion obsolete?

About 3,300 years ago Moses put together the main elements of Judaism which later served as the basis for Christianity and to some extent, later still, for Islam. Therefore, by focusing on Judaism *Exodus to Humanism* offers a lead to Christians and even to Moslems as well, because if Judaism is obsolete, so also Christianity and to some extent Islam are obsolete.

The main point made is that the Jews should no longer rely on the religion of Judaism for the survival of their identity precisely because if the Jewish identity relies on the obsolete religion of Judaism, sooner or later the Jewish identity will be obsolete.

I argue the point by describing how and why I and twenty-seven Jewish contributors either never believed in the religion of Judaism or rejected it at some stage in our lives. I was born in Israel, the son of a man who devoted his life (and his money) for the creation of a new Israeli *secular* state in the ancestral land of the Jewish people.

The object of *Exodus to Humanism* is not to preach to the converted, but rather to engage in a dialogue with the millions of the indifferent, the undecided, the "don't knows," and the "don't cares" who just carry on pretending to believe without any real conviction.

This book is not really about fighting Judaism in particular and religion in general. This book is about *replacing* Judaism and religion with what readers feel ought to replace them.

To readers: After having read this book, please do not hesitate to e-mail your comments, ideas, and suggestions to: Exodtohumanism@ btinternet.com.

David Ibry
December 1998

Introduction

Why this book?

For centuries upon centuries the Jews have been dreaming of returning to the land of their forefathers. Every year the Passover Seder (the Last Supper of Jesus Christ) ended with the ritual promise of celebrating the Passover in Jerusalem the following year. Finally, in the second half of the nineteenth century a new movement started. There was something different in this new movement for the return of the Jewish people to the land of Zion: *it was not a religious movement.* It broke away from the traditional approach of every Jewish movement for the last eighteen hundred years and it broke away from the eastern European culture where it was born, which had not yet absorbed the secular ideology of western Europe.

By the end of the nineteenth century the political vision of Zionism had taken an increasing hold of the minds of eastern European Jewry. Some Jews, for example, my father, devoted their lives and their money to its realization.

Today, more than fifty years after the establishment of the state of Israel, the time is ripe for the Israelis and for Jews the world over to confront the modern world from the new reality in the history of the

Jewish people, placing the Jews in the same position with regard to
religion as all other nationalities.

The purpose of this book is to help the Jews worldwide and the
Israelis to come to terms with a new role and a new identity entirely
separate from religion. In my opinion, in our day and age a clear-cut
and unequivocal separation between Jewishness and the obsolete religion of Judaism, traumatic as it may seem, is nevertheless a fundamental conceptual step the Jews will have to take, because if the
Jewish identity were to rely, in our day and age, on the obsolete religion of Judaism, sooner or later Jewishness would be obsolete. *And
according to the original Zionist dream, the lead should have come
from the new Jewish state of Israel.*

From a Life Story to a Book

The more I wrote my story the more I felt the wish to find out about
other stories, other experiences of humanists with a Jewish background, with whom I could share the drama of a break from beliefs
and religious rituals which had been an integral part of the Jewish
identity for about 3,300 years. So I put an announcement in the
Humanist News of the British Humanist Association. The response
was overwhelming: not so much because of the number of replies, but
because of the intensity of the feelings in the replies. The ways each
of them interpreted their identity were so varied that I was faced with
the problem of defining, in my own mind, nonreligious Jewishness.

I looked for a common denominator, but the only one I could find
was condemnation for the suffering forced on people by the arrogance
of religious dogma. There were the moving stories of those forced to
conform to different identities, like Olga, who survived the Holocaust
in Poland by pretending and living as a Christian and now "feels
Jewish only because the anti-Semites say so." There were others who
wrote of their anger when rejected by fellow Jews, and there were
those who refused to be indicted as lacking an identity by other Jews
who still believe in a set of outdated, senseless, and ridiculous religious tenets.

A few expressed feelings of animosity at the sight of believers praying to *their God* and there were also those born in a humanist environment from humanist Jewish parents who had not faced any traumatic break with orthodox traditions. The interesting point is that though they were not brought up to believe in Judaism, they were holding on to their Jewishness. But most seemed to agree that all religions are inevitably destined to become less and less relevant and that this is bound to create problems for the Jewish identity in the Diaspora.

There also were reservations about mentioning Israel in the introduction of this book. Though I and all the contributors deplore the present policies of the Israeli government, to my mind, the existence of Israel will produce a huge impact on Jewish culture and identity throughout the world. To me this is not a political pro-Israeli let alone a Zionist statement, but simply a statement of a factual reality. Though at present the old world of Judaism has successfully hijacked the new state of Israel, hopefully Israel will eventually become a modern secular country for the Jews who retain a Jewish identity to look up to, as a cultural model.

So I decided my best course was to gather the life stories describing the experiences, feelings, and conclusions of other humanists with a Jewish background and produce a book which rejects the notion that the Jewish identity needs to be based on religious norms and beliefs. In fact, I believe that the preservation of a Jewish identity in the Diaspora will be based on how the Diaspora Jews will retain their Jewishness without believing in the religion of Judaism. Though I found it impossible to offer a definition of Jewishness without Judaism, I had to find a way to open the book by expressing what Jewishness means to Jews who do not follow or believe in Judaism.

Jewishness Without Judaism, or To Be a Jew in 1998

As the Holocaust has such a dramatic prominence in Jewish and world history, I include **Prof. Jean-Claude Pecker**'s contribution in the introduction. Professor Pecker is a world-renowned astronomer and member of the Academie Nationale, the Academie Royale Belgique, and the Academie European of Science.

"From a tender age, as far as I can remember, I knew I was a Jew. My parents had told me: 'You are a Jew, just like both of us, like your grandparents, the parents of your grandparents, and so on from generation to generation. But you are not following the religion of Judaism, because for us the Bible is but a series of beautiful legends. For us it is neither a historical document with any real historical value, nor a holy book which defines the only truth and its laws. . . . We do not believe in God or in the afterlife of a soul. And we believe that all religions ought to renounce their dogmatic claims and acknowledge instead that all humans share the same human destiny. Like Voltaire we fight against and abhor intolerance. Though we are Jews, we do not follow the laws of Moses. We do not celebrate the day of Atonement, or Purim, or any other religious festival. We eat pork and veal cooked in its mother's milk. . . . However, having made that clear, we also state that we do not deny our Jewishness!'

"My maternal grandfather, an Alsatian who chose France in 1871, was a chief rabbi who had been stoned at the time of the Dreyfus case. In 1914, when already old, he volunteered to defend France in World War I. My other grandfather, a doctor who had left the Ukraine to escape pogroms and persecution around 1880, also volunteered in 1914.

"Before World War II my parents and I lived in Bordeaux. We had no Jewish friends, and even at high school I had no Jewish schoolmates. I was a scout, but a Protestant scout . . . and in 1936 I took part in street battles in support of the Popular Front, against those who shouted 'Death to Blum and to the Jews!' So, even without believing in Judaism, I felt part of the Jewish antifascist struggle.

"Then war came. . . . In Paris I was a boarder at the Saint-Louis Grammar High School . . . with a yellow Star of David on my suit and a red rubber stamp on my identity card marking me as JEW. I was probably the only student in the Ecole Normale in the Rue d'Ulm, having passed my entry examination in 1942, with a yellow star on my suit. A little while after that exam I was in Grenoble. The Jewish refugees from Paris filled half the lecture room. A division was already emerging within the group of the people entrapped in the net. There were those who were choosing a new clandestine identity and were joining the Maquis* and on

---

*The French partisans who fought the German occupation.

the other side those who shouted, 'Maréchal, nous voilà!' (Field Marshal Pétain, here we are!)* But how could one know? Whom could one trust? In Bordeaux I had no Jewish friends, but in Grenoble I had only Jewish friends. Many have disappeared. Life in hiding followed and then, in 1944, it was June when my father and my mother were despatched by cattle train to Auschwitz.

"They never came back, like millions of others. How could one ever forget all that?

"Having said that, I must add that I feel far from Israel. My grand-parents, Jews who had chosen France, who had fought for the values of the French secular Republic, never considered Zionism as a valid alternative. My rabbi grandfather was opposed to it on religious grounds. Of course, when after the war it was necessary to find asylum for the 'displaced persons' (what a sad euphemism), Israel seemed to offer a solution. As far as I am concerned, although I feel Jewish, I reject the religion of Judaism just like any other religion. I am French and I wish to remain French for as long as possible.

"Because who knows the future? Who knows if one day those who threw stones at my grandfather, those who condemned Dreyfus, the children of Drumont and Maurras, those who hailed Petain, those who vote for the National Front, those who are after my skin, will again be in power? If that were to happen, I would have to go into exile and it is precisely this constant threat, for centuries upon centuries, in country after country, which builds up the feeling of being Jewish and of solidarity with other Jews. Sartre or Memmi realized it. It is anti-Semitism which feeds the consciousness of being Jewish!"

The Problem of Defining Jewishness as Separate from Judaism

Prof. Evry Schatzman, a leading world researcher in astrophysics and a member of the French Academy of Sciences, contributes a clear analysis of how he separates Jewishness from the religion of Judaism.

*Field Marshal Philippe Pétain (1856–1951), a French hero of World War I, was the head of state of the Vichy government, which collaborated with the German occupiers.

"My father, carried away to Auschwitz in 1941 and exterminated in 1942, was a committed atheist, but nevertheless he felt strongly that he belonged to the Jewish community.

"I was brought up as an atheist, and *my being Jewish and my feelings about being Jewish are based on the fact that my parents were Jewish*. During the war my Jewish wife and I had survived living in hiding with false names and later brought up our three children as nonbelievers. However, my daughter, though a nonbeliever, respects some Jewish traditions and festivals, and her daughter (my granddaughter), perhaps trying to solve the contradiction, emigrated to Israel.

"If I try to analyze what my Jewishness means to me, I am led to the concepts of citizenship, nationality, and ethnicity. One could be French and at the same time a Breton, a Corsican, or a Basque. One could also be French and an atheist or a Protestant or an Orthodox Jew. When I feel that I belong to an entity which I define as an ethnic entity for lack of any better term, it does not mean that I entertain social, political, or ideological relationships with the other members of that entity. For me, this ethnic entity is not a racial entity, and my feeling of belonging is certainly rather a confused feeling, but social situations could rekindle it.

"I am not going to express any opinion about the desirability of the survival of the Jewish identity. To hold onto links with Jews who follow the religion of Judaism is an entirely individual affair, because it reflects deep emotional needs which vary from person to person. As far as I am concerned, I have not tried to hold onto such links. My relationships with Jews in and out of France relate to informal or family occasions. Therefore I have no strong belief about the desirability of the survival of a Jewish identity entirely separate from the religion of Judaism. For me, to celebrate Pesah (the Jewish Passover) with my children and grandchildren is not a religious ritual; it is simply a way to remember that I belong to what I call an ethnicity, by celebrating its legendary history."

Having Rejected the Religion of Judaism, Are Jews Left with an Identity Problem?

Mrs. Olga Faroqui was born Olga Grossfeld in Poland in 1927. Both her father and mother were doctors. "They were nonbelievers" and she and her brother she writes "were brought up as such." Her parents separated when she was five years old. This is her story:

"I didn't go to school but was taught at home. The alternative would have been a Polish state school with its huge dose of Catholicism and where most certainly we would have been subject to anti-Semitic remarks by other pupils. In the town there was also a Jewish orthodox school, but this did not appeal to my nonreligious mother either. . . .

"At the start of the war we went east to escape the advancing German army. We reached Lvov, a city in eastern Poland, now in Ukraine. We stayed there in a flat belonging to my mother's cousin. For two years, from 1939 to 1941, Lvov was part of the Soviet Union. There I went to school, at last! For many years afterward I remembered those as the happiest years in my life. It didn't seem to matter that we lived in one room sharing bathroom and kitchen facilities with other refugee families. All these were small inconveniences compared with the fact that I went to school. Not only this: I had a friend. Her name was Janina [Jane] Ehrlich. We were inseparable and spent all our spare time together.

"In 1941 the truce between Germany and the Soviet Union ended and the Germans occupied Lvov. After a few months they created a ghetto in the city. All the Jews had to live there. We were allowed to leave the ghetto during the day, but we had to wear armbands with Stars of David embroidered on them, and we had to be back before a certain time in the evening. The conditions in the ghetto were bad. It was overcrowded and there was little food. But the worst was the general sense of impending disaster. Our mother tried to keep a brave face for our sake. But I remember that when I was visiting Jane I used to find her mother in tears, saying things like, 'What is the point of trying to obtain food and preparing it so that it is tasty when they are going to kill us anyway?'

"I don't remember exactly how long we stayed in the ghetto; a few months, I think. Then my mother organized escape for us. A young Polish woman provided us with false identity documents. Her name was Helena Zachaczewska. She had helped other Jews, too. Several years after the war I received a letter from Israel asking me to certify that she had saved our lives. On the basis of mine and other testimonies she was later invited to Israel and presented with the title of righteous gentile. She then planted a commemorative tree at a special ceremony.

"Equipped with the documents we walked out of the ghetto knowing that this time we were not going to return. Outside we entered a dark staircase of a block of flats and discarded our armbands. We were now Poles with a very Polish name of Swierszczewski. We walked to the railway station, where we met Helena who took us to her native village, where we were to spend the rest of the war. Because of the necessary secrecy I was not even allowed to say goodbye to Jane. I never saw her again. We learned later that the whole population of the ghetto was taken to the concentration camp and killed in the gas chambers.

"Nobody in the village suspected that we were Jews. At that time many Poles came from the towns to the villages, as it was safer and cheaper to live there. On Sundays everybody went to Church and we had to go, too, so as not to arouse suspicion. We also went to confession!

"As a result I am quite familiar with the Catholic religion, but know next to nothing about Judaism. The Catholic mass, with the rich garments of the priests, the ringing bells, the incomprehensible Latin, was designed to induce awe and fear of God. Not to mention the sermons with the constant threat of Hell. At the impressionable age of fifteen I was for a while beginning to have doubts. Then one night, during a violent storm, I did an experiment. I repeated in a whisper 'I don't believe in God, I don't believe in God,' half thinking that if there were a God he would punish me and strike me with lightning.

"But nothing happened.

"We spent about three years in the village, helping with the work on the farm and, as far as I was concerned, enjoying the countryside. Somehow I did not fully realize the seriousness of our situation, the danger we were in. I suppose it was the optimism of youth. I never doubted that the war would end with the German defeat and that we would survive. Only later did I understand under what enormous stress my mother must have been during those years. Not only was I certain that we would survive, I also naively imagined that after the war the world would be a better place than it was before. It seemed then that Nazism was the only evil, and once this was conquered people would live in peace and harmony forever.

"I was sharply brought down to reality after the Red Army entered the village. I was talking to a young man from the village whom I thought of as well mannered, kind, and intelligent. In the course of conversation he said: 'I am glad that the Germans lost the war, but one good thing that Hitler did was to kill all those Jews.' I should have told him who I was. I should at least have objected in the strongest terms. I said nothing. I was afraid. . . .

"I feel that I don't belong. Being a nonbeliever rules out a religious community. Who am I? Am I Jewish because of my 'blood'? Am I Polish because of the culture and language I know best? Am I British because of my citizenship? I feel that I am all and none of these things.

"I imagine that it must be nice to belong to a community. It gives one a sense of identity and security. But there is a very thin line between this and saying: 'We are better than them.' So I would rather remain who I am: a human being."

The crux of the matter is to provide a logical answer to the question: *Why would the Diaspora Jews who have rejected the religion of Judaism want to retain a separate and exclusive Jewish identity?*

Professor Emeritus Paul Kurtz, the distinguished academic from New York, writes in *Free Inquiry* (Summer 1997): "We should encourage intermarriage, miscegenation and other such processes, but especially the creation of secular societies, which encourage people of diverse ethnicities to settle and live together and to transcend the ancient loyalties of the past . . . [because] from the secular humanist perspective, assimilation is a positive good and is not to be feared. The moral agenda for humanists is to persuade people that we need to go beyond the ancient divisive loyalties of the past and to attain a new ethical level in which all persons become a part of the community of humankind. This may be difficult. But if it is happening in America, why not elsewhere?"

However, there also are humanist Jews who, although without faith in the religion of Judaism, do not wish to give up their Jewish identity.

Professor Emeritus Sir Isaiah Berlin wrote to me: "I do not merely consider myself to be a Jew, but I am one—I am a Jew in the same sense as I have two arms, two legs, two eyes, etc. . . . I regard it without question as natural to me and part of my identity."

Perhaps trying to clear my own ideas with regard to a Diaspora Jewishness entirely independent from the religion of Judaism, I asked **Professor Emeritus Sir Hermann Bondi,** the president of the British Humanist Association, for his opinion.

"You ask a very interesting question," he wrote to me, "and my response involves the question how a Jewish identity manifests itself. I would never deny my Jewishness and take a real interest in my ancestry. *These feelings are quite separate from any belief in Judaism.*"

So, having rejected the religion of Judaism and its criteria about Jewishness, it appears to me that we are left with two views of one's Jewishness: the way one perceives himself or herself, and the way others perceive him or her. The two views are closely interrelated because the way we perceive ourselves is, to a very large extent, determined by the way others perceive us and in turn others depend on us, at least to some extent, for how they perceive us.

The thesis of this book is that Jewishness is separate from adherence to the religion of Judaism. Ideally, Jewishness in the Diaspora should be about the way one feels and not about complying with whatever rules and following whatever religious regulations. Because whereas following the religion of Judaism, as for all religions, ought to be a matter of belief and not a matter of having one or both Jewish parents, the feeling of sharing the values of the great Jewish cultural tradition and its history of achievement and persecution ought to be a matter of a person's sentiment.

But how would the half-believing indifferent millions of Diaspora Jews, and all those not really following the rules of Judaism, react to such a thesis? Would they feel threatened? Antagonized? Diminished?

*   *   *

Howard Gross is a successful London solicitor. Though in fact a nonbeliever, he is not a humanist. After reading the first six pages of this introduction he wrote to me: "I do not believe in a god . . . [but] I have no objection to people who believe in a religion and I do not despise them. . . . I find that believers are too often intolerant . . . [but], with respect, your remarks about an 'obsolete' religion are just as intolerant as any made by a believer."

Is humanism being intolerant because it dares to state its views and in the process exposes religion? Judaism, as a religion, is based on God and on the special relationship between God and the children of Israel. In the world of yesteryear many needed religion for an explanation which would help them to figure out what life was all about. In our day and age religion can survive only through acrobatic compromises with our real world.

But an identity problem is still there because Mr. Gross continues: "When asked how I reconciled being a Jew and a nonbeliever, . . . I would wish to turn the question on its head, because for me the conflict has always been—how I can reconcile being both a Jew and an Englishman? . . . No, my problem is that my hairs stand up, eyes water, not just when I hear Sophie Tucker sing (in Yiddish) 'My Yddisher Mama,' when Kaddish is sung for the Holocaust victims, but also when I read of 'the Thin Red Line,' of Waterloo, the Somme, Magna Carta, the Battle of Hastings. I am as proud of the English parliamentary democracy as of the great Jewish contribution to civilization. England is my football team, Israel my concern."

Here we have it: people's identities are in fact determined by their feelings!

And now I wish to quote one sentence from the contribution of **Josh Kutchinsky** to chapter 8: "Let me answer the question: Am I a Jew? Well, in stereotypical fashion I will answer a question with a question. So, just because I don't believe in God you want me to disown my ancestors among whom were individuals as great as any of the greatest cathedral builders? The cultural cathedral that is Jewishness is too rich in beauty and too steeped in blood to disown."

A New Exodus?

In the course of a conversation a contributor pointed out to me that the tenets of Judaism, the Ten Commandments, the Toràh, were all subsequent to the Exodus of the Hebrews from Egypt. "Yes," I said, "but even if all the accounts and all the 613 precepts were written down after the Exodus, surely there must have been even before the Exodus some set of beliefs in an exclusive deity of their own which distinguished the Hebrews from the Egyptians."

The Hebrews were different because, to start with, they spoke a different language, probably akin to the Semitic language of the Hyksos who ruled for a short while over Egypt, and obviously the Hebrews had different folk myths, different customs, and their own deity, because they were a different people who had developed their own individual identity in an another country.

As the Hebrews moved out of Egypt following the footsteps of the Hyksos, they structured their religious folk myths into a full-fledged religion with properly defined beliefs and clear-cut rules and regulations. Probably at this time they felt the need to place their religion with its rules and regulations on record and were able to achieve this by adopting their version of the Ugarit alphabet.*

The first priority was to define their old mythological deity and place it in an unassailable position, well above any other deity and commanding such a high level of respect that no Hebrew would dare commit blasphemy. (Why at that time was blasphemy considered the greatest sin, the object of a commandment? Most probably the old proverb "familiarity breeds contempt" offers a clue.)

The names of the folk myths and of the deity of the Hebrews who dwelt in Egypt, like the myths of all peoples of antiquity, must have had some meaning in their Semitic language even before they were able to write them. After the Exodus, when in the Sinai the Hebrews started formulating and writing down the structures of their religion,

---

*Some research points to Ugarit having been the first alphabet around 1200 B.C.E. If this were the case then the laws of Moses in the Sinai must have been written in Hieratic or Demotic Egyptian script.

they had to write with their new alphabet the name of their old deity and the one sure way to prevent any chance of blasphemy was by keeping its name unknown.

As Hebrew is written without vowels* and as since the destruction of the second temple in 71 C.E., we have not received any indication of how that unknown name was pronounced only once a year by the High Priest on the day of the Atonement in the Temple of Jerusalem, its actual pronunciation is a matter of guesswork. Many assumed it to be *Yehova*, but other scholars assume it to be *Yahve*. Both names have no meaning in Hebrew. According to my hypothesis the correct pronunciation is *Yahvò*, which meant "It will come."† The significance of my hypothesis is that *Yahvò* was a future-oriented deity performing the most essential task of divining the unknown future.

Yahvò will not help us to a second Exodus. Those Jews who will want to retain their Jewish identity in the Diaspora, will have to do so without it. However, *Yahvò* may still give a lead on how best to improve the present by focusing on the future rather than the past. And if the Exodus started it all, a new Exodus may offer a lead to Christians as well and perhaps also to Muslims.

The Significance of a New Exodus for Christianity

The Holy Mass, which the Aramaic-speaking Christians adopted as their main ritual in the Roman catacombs, repeats the celebration of the Seder of Jesus Christ with his disciples in Jerusalem before his crucifixion. The Seder is a ritual meal rehearsing the Exodus, and in this way *the rehearsal of the Exodus constitutes the most important ritual of Judaism as well as of Christianity*. The Jewish Seder teaches the

---

*Archaic alphabets mimic the ontogenesis of speech and speech was based on the ability of uttering and combining consonants.

†"To come" is spelled with ב and not with ו. However the Hebrew alphabet, like many archaic languages and alphabets, did not differentiate between the pronunciation of B and V. My theory to explain why *Yahvò* is spelled with ו is the subject of a separate research. *Its main point is that in personal names* ב *is interchangeable with* ו, *as in Bat-sheva.*

young and reminds the adults of the time when Judaism came into being during the hard struggle to survive (for a couple of generations) in the desolate and inhospitable Sinai desert. It was at that time that the Seder was first structured and its celebration became an essential part of the rituals of the new religion.

What was its meaning to the early Christians in Rome? Having grown up as Jews and being aliens in Rome, they clung to their Jewish identity as a means of retaining their self-respect in an environment where they were probably looked down on as lesser persons who could not speak proper Latin. They looked back at Jerusalem and not to Rome as the center of the Christian world.

Until the Council of Nicaea in 325, the Christians celebrated Easter on the same date as the Jewish Passover and called it *Pasha,* or *Pasqua* in the Latin alphabet. (*Pasha* is Aramaic for the Hebrew *Pesah,* which is the name for Passover in Hebrew, and *Pasqua* is still the Italian for Easter.)

In my opinion humanism will never get hold of large sections of the population without a framework of rituals and what better ritual than one based on a humanist Exodus which could embrace Jews as well as Christians?

Many humanists assume that we are rational beings and that therefore we would progress by living, behaving, and believing only in what is assumed to be rational. But I believe that we are not the rational beings we think we are and that more often than not we in fact call rational what is for us the right and correct way to be, *because we just could not be, if we were not emotional beings.* Our so-called survival drive is not a logical process. If we were to start by acknowledging and accepting what we really are and then build upon it, we might realize our emotional need for rituals.

In the United States and the United Kingdom, as in all so-called Christian countries, nonbelievers, agnostics, atheists, and humanists cannot avoid taking some part in the Christian holidays. Should humanists with a Jewish as well as Christian background celebrate an Easter/Passover where the values and the struggles of humanism are remembered?

1

My Case for Humanism

Fighting the TRUTH

My earliest memories are about the TRUTH.

Doda Lena* was sitting next to me in our garden on the slopes of Mt. Carmel. Her voice was soft and melodious. She had large grey eyes and a bony, angular body. She must have been an attractive young woman, but to me she was an ageless aunt whose purpose in life was to be nice to me and tell me stories.

There was peace and security in that Israeli garden. My father was probably reading in his library, my mother was busy organizing our meal with Yona, the maid, and my sister was still at the Reali primary school.

It was a long story: this young man, Doda Lena told me, was seeking the TRUTH. At first he believed it to be among the Goyim (the Gentiles), but later he discovered other Goyim with a better TRUTH.

---

*Miss Helena Constance Frank, daughter of Dr. Philip Frank and Lady Agnes neè Grosvenor, daughter of Richard Grosvenor the second Marquess of Westminster. Doda Lena's mother was probably the first English blueblood related to the royal family to marry a Jew.

Eventually after searching left, right, and center throughout the whole world, he finally realized where the real TRUTH lay: here with us, because it was the same TRUTH we believed in—my father, Doda Lena, myself, my sister, our neighbors and their children.

Of my father's death, I only remember that day. The grave was a mound of reddish soil,* and we all stood around it. I was not crying. I think nobody was crying, but I had a strange feeling that people were supposed to cry, though I was not sure why. And I sensed that my mother was somehow different and later on I heard her speaking differently.

I remember how I enjoyed the trip on the big white ship, the marine breeze, and the occasional splash of salty taste. In the evenings we had Tarzan films on deck. To me it seemed a huge boat on an endless sea, and I was sorry when we reached land and had to leave that endless sea.

In the new Italian home they spoke differently. I felt ashamed because I could only speak with my mother and my sister. I had already learned some rudiments of writing, but now my mother taught us how to write differently. We were told that what we knew was Hebrew and what we were learning was Italian.

There were many exciting new things around the new house and in fact I did not mind the change, although I missed the garden and the long hours spent watching the ants and the spiders.

Also I felt somewhat uneasy at being different.

We lived with Grandmother, Auntie, and Auntie's daughter. It was Grandmother who made me feel uneasy. I admired her sitting there at the head of the table, always so straight and composed (of course I didn't know she was wearing a corset).

She hardly ever smiled and I do not recall having ever seen her laughing. For her, things were either black or white, either truly right—and that meant Roman Catholic dogma—or truly wrong, whatever was not Roman Catholic.

I would have liked her to approve of me because I realized that

---

*The red soil of Benyamina, in what is now Israel, where my father was buried in 1933.

there was something about me which was not the way it should have been. I cannot put it into words; presumably I just wanted to be like the others, to have been born in a place like the others, and yes, to be a Christian like the others.

When the anti-Jewish laws were announced, emotionally they brought nothing new to me. All "those" feelings were already part of my world, a world of insecurity and isolation. The novelty was that now I had to be ashamed, now I had to forget that faraway house and its garden. I had to hide their existence deep in my memory, so I tried not to think about them anymore.

Because of the new laws I could no longer attend state schools, and my mother sent me to a private school run by the Jesuits. There I received a very thorough tuition in the TRUTH.

My cousin Carlo was older than me. He was how I should have been. He had nothing to hide; he was born in the right place and people liked him. It was my cousin who taught me the facts of life. I was shocked and could hardly believe it. My mother and grandmother never spoke about the facts of life and I understood that there was something improper about them. My cousin told me of when he asked a girl to go to the movies with him. I envied him, though I was not clear about what I would have liked to do with a girl at the movies.

We had Mass every morning at the Institute of the Jesuits. When Padre Tessarolo thundered from the pulpit warning us against impure thoughts leading to impure acts, a light flashed in my mind. Suddenly I knew what I would have liked to do with Ines if I had dared to ask her to come to the movies with me and if she had accepted. (Ines was our housemaid and of course much older than me.) There in the darkness I would have searched for her breasts and . . . yes, this was exactly what I was not supposed to think about, as Padre Tessarolo warned us. It was my first confrontation with the TRUTH, or better it was just that parts of me were sort of unwilling to conform with the TRUTH.

Most nights when I went to bed a big fight raged in my mind between parts of me which were "evil" and the TRUTH. At times evil was too strong and won the day, or rather the night.

It took me years before I started doubting the TRUTH.

The newspapers, the radio, the large street posters were all continuously dishing out TRUTHS. Even though the TRUTHS dished out by the papers and the radio were not the same kind of TRUTHS Padre Tessarolo was thundering about, they were equally presented as TRUTHS one *should not* and *could not* doubt.

I am not sure how and when it happened. I can't say if it had been a sudden or a slow process, if anyone or anything in particular had influenced me. The fact is that I grasped something new which I found very stimulating: the concept of my ability to think with my own head, and my power to reject any claim to lay down the law about the TRUTH of right and wrong.

Religion

If I want to be logically consistent in challenging the truth, I have to focus on religion, because religion is based on a message of truth.

Whereas human theories on whatever subject—social, moral, political, and even scientific ideologies—are open to human challenge and doubt, religion offers superhuman messages which are revealed to humanity through channels designated by a power no human can challenge. Well then, how do you explain all those intelligent and clever people believing absurd and utter nonsense, performing irrational rituals and being mesmerized into a world of fiction and make-believe. The answer is simple: through indoctrination and conditioning, usually from a very early age. Parents, educators, ruling classes, and political leaders all feel the need for a covenant with supernatural powers in order to secure discipline, law, and order by means of superhuman rules which should not be disobeyed and could not be doubted.

Perhaps, after all, I had been lucky because the unusual circumstances of my life helped me to reject all such claims of exclusive truths on the part of religions.

I imagine that at the beginning religions were a tribal affair. A tribe was held together by and derived its self-confidence and strength from its religion. Wars were a matter of a religion with its god or gods against another religion with its own god or gods. Much later when the

Roman Empire adopted Christianity, religion was used to enforce *morally* the allegiance of its many and diverse subjects. *Moral* being the key word, because it meant that people had to follow whatever rules out of an inner compulsion prevailing over other human feelings and impulses.

Models

My problem was that I needed a model to look up to, an ideal to aim at and identify with. At the Leone XIII, the Institute of the Jesuits, they taught me that the meek will inherit the earth and that the last will be first. Surely, I thought to myself, if the meek and the last achieve greater merit, this implies some hierarchical order where people are considered more or less than others. So, if I were to model myself on the last rather than the first, it would be my way of trying to excel by being better than others, which appears to defeat the message of the model.

Whatever model, it seems to be based on more or less of some value. Is this what all humans have in common: the ambition to achieve more, i.e., to achieve more than others, because no one could be more unless somebody else were less?

My only teacher not wearing the habit was De Simoni. He was a lieutenant in the fascist militia and taught us military culture. Though the Institute was a private school and therefore able to accept me notwithstanding the anti-Jewish laws, when it came to the syllabus they had to conform with the official curriculum as set out by the Ministry of Education.

De Simoni was a handsome young man, always immaculately dressed in the fascist uniform. He talked well and convincingly. Often he reminded us of Mussolini's slogan: *Better a Single Day as a Lion Than a Hundred Days as a Sheep*. Almost in the same breath he would warn us of a major danger facing the world: a conspiracy by international Judaism allied with international Communism and international capitalist freemasonry. Every time he said that, it felt like being physically attacked, because I knew that he *knew,* and I knew that the whole class *knew*. As soon as his lesson started, I dreaded what was to come.

I wished somebody, perhaps my father or just anyone, would come to my side. I wished I had the courage to be a lion and jump on my desk and stand up to them and have the guts to shout them down. But I didn't. If there was such a thing as God, it would have been on their side. I was on my own and I could rely only on myself.

I was growing up and I was afraid. I was not afraid of God and I was not afraid of Hell. I feared men, what they could do for the sake of whatever theoretical construction they had built up in their own minds.

To feel safe I needed strength, and strength is but the result of a rapport where the strong are strong inasmuch as others are weaker; and my condition was making others strong at my expense. In order to face by myself all those people judging me through their whichever loyalties and whichever set of entrenched truths, I had to rely on something offering me the strength to stand up to them and challenge their truths.

O God of Israel

Oh God of Israel, hast thou not heard the cries of the mothers, the screams of the children, hast thou not seen thy people being exterminated?

During the last period of the war, when northern Italy was occupied by the Germans, we moved out to the countryside, and though we didn't know about the extermination camps, we realized how dangerous and life-threatening was the situation for me. I had false identity papers with a different name and place of birth. It made me tense, and I developed an inner anxiety at the sight of anyone in a military or police uniform, because people were often stopped and asked to identify themselves. I understand now that I owe my life to all those who guessed or knew, but did not report me. There was a reward for anyone reporting Jews to the authorities, and not far away, on Lake Maggiore, the Germans were led to the villas of Jews. The Germans killed them and then threw their bodies in the lake before ransacking the villas. Writing about those days now, after more than fifty years, after having seen and experienced so much more than at that time, I wish to express my appreciation and gratitude to the society which surrounded me, for its great humanity.

Eventually the war ended. I no longer had to hide my identity, nor to lie or pretend about myself. One thing I had learned: to mistrust those who claim to know the real truth and feel justified to force it on others. There were two major truths in postwar Europe. Naturally they both claimed and preached how superior their own truth was. Though only one truth claimed to have God on its side, the other one acted as if it were a religious theocracy, preventing and suffocating by violent means all attempts of different, let alone contrary ideologies. Deep down I was still looking for something to believe in, and I did not appreciate my fortunate position. My life had been so much affected by unforeseen events that I was seeking the certainty in correct values as a way of coping with the anxiety caused by possible new and unknown circumstances.

We are born Christians or Jews, Protestants or Catholics, etc., and we are brainwashed accordingly about moral, sociological, and national correctness. When we meet others brainwashed with different sets of correct values, we are pushed into reinforcing our own correct values, in order to fight off what is sensed as a threat to a fundamental part of our identity, on which we rely for our psychological security. I know now that correctness should express the ways, the behavior, the rules we should live by, and not the ways, the behavior, the rules we are told and instructed to live by. The problem is, how can we see through the indoctrination we have received and identify the rules we should live by?

The answer must be that it is for society to debate, decide, and set out the rules the majority want to live by. This means that it is not up to any ruling authority, civilian or ecclesiastical, to decide and proclaim the moral rules, but instead it is for society to debate and then express a majority decision over its own moral laws. Only by refusing to be locked into whatever lager (guarded encampment) of whatever correctness was I finally able to feel stronger than those who are locked in their respective lagers.

Okay, it gave me an exhilarating feeling of freedom to realize that I could decide not to abide by whatever rules of whatever lager without incurring the wrath of whatever supernatural power. But if societies need rules and regulations in order to function and survive, as a member of society don't I have to abide by the rules and regulations of my society?

Morality

from

X   ~~Since~~ birth we learn and are taught what is good or bad for our well-being and for our survival. Sooner rather than later we absorb a reality which has to be coped with by means of rules and norms. And all those rules and norms imply dichotomous value judgments about what is right or wrong.

Presumably one of the very first problems for an organized social life was the validation of whatever rules and norms regulated it. The rules and norms about the fundamental rights and wrongs have to be made so definitely certain that they become part of one's own way of seeing things. The easiest validation was by means of a revelation from some superhuman source, which in turn would require a religious structure to justify it.

When I think of explaining the power of religion, I think about my grandmother. She was a remarkable person, but with hindsight I realize that her unshakable certainty of being right and her absolute refusal to consider the possibility of being wrong ended up by building feelings of resentment in me.

The trouble with religious systems of morality is precisely their claim of perfect truth for their moral values. Like all values, true values express a dichotomy where they are negated by opposite values, because if good was not contrasted by bad and all was good, then good would cease to be of any value. But, whereas moral values produced by humans are only relative to given human circumstances and are negated by opposite values relative to the same human circumstances, the superhuman values of religions have to be negated by a superhuman absolute evil. On the one hand superhuman absolutely true values offer to believers the psychological confidence of being absolutely right, but on the other hand human progress is made possible by doubt and lack of certainty. Furthermore, in interhuman affairs, the certainty of being absolutely right leads to the highest possible level of emotional confrontation.

Moral judgments are human psychological constructions through which we achieve the kind of intellectual structural order in our perception of reality, granting us positive feelings about ourselves, our views, and our behavior. Well, the proof of the pudding is in the eating and as one cannot claim that good always prevails, the moral systems of religions rely on the support of an ideal perfect world. And without the support of a perfect world, I seemed destined to face a lonely and difficult existential battle.

Humanism

What a relief, what a great joy when I discovered that there were thousands upon thousands sharing my views. Prominent persons, learned ones, and people in all walks of life. For me humanism is a human worldview, or rather a worldview of how humans explain, interpret, and make sense of our reality. And this means that we have to accept that our ideals, however dear they are to us, have to be taken with buckets of salt.

Francesco Petrarca (1304–1374)—Petrarch—is considered the first great humanist. At that time, when royals had libraries of about fifty manuscripts, Petrarch had a library of about two hundred. He was very keen not only to read the literary works of the great Roman civilization, but also to figure out what made that civilization great, how it functioned, what its people believed and thought.

Petrarch, though a Christian believer, was a scholar in *Studia Humanitatis,* the studies concerning humankind on earth rather than the supernatural world of theological studies. When admiring the pagan civilization of Rome and Greece, he felt empathy for the Roman way of life and its values. On the surface it may appear that the basic theoretical difference between the three great monotheistic religions—Judaism, Christianity, and Islam—and the paganism of Rome and Greece is that whereas the monotheistic religions have only one God, the Romans and the Greeks had plenty: ten, twenty, or however many more. *In fact there is a much deeper difference of substance besides numbers.*

The Roman and Greek gods, though immortal and very powerful, were humanlike, with all the passions, weaknesses, feelings, loves, hates, jealousies, pleasures, and displeasures of the senses of humans. In other words, they were not perfect; they were fallible and *could make mistakes*. So in the pagan Roman and Greek world, the model for absolute perfection was practically absent. This pagan way of looking at reality did not make humans any more or any less wicked, but it removed the possibility of covering up human mistakes, human wickedness, and human nonsense with *perfectly true* dogma which cannot be doubted.

Petrarch was a poet and not a philosopher. He was a man of feelings and not of theories and probably never bothered to rationalize with logical argument his empathy for the pagan values of ancient Rome. And in any case, in the late Middle Ages challenging religion and the Church would have been no joke and people would have refrained from expressing openly whatever doubts they might have harbored in their minds.

As a student of Italian literature at university, I felt drawn to Petrarch. It dawned on me that the correct way for understanding was by admitting the imperfection in our capacity to postulate a perfect God. I asked myself: if Petrarch had achieved this view, what had motivated him? Perhaps looking around a countryside ravaged by barbarian foreign militias where the monuments of the ancient Roman glory stood derelict and defaced, Petrarch tried to resurrect what he saw as his own heritage, the great civilization of his ancestors.

Religion and Identity

I could not get rid of feelings of guilt at not being as my father would have wanted me to be. He would have wanted me to be living, working, and fighting for his dream of a new Zion. Even before settling in Israel, he had changed his Jewish Russian name into the most Hebrew name he could think of. Notwithstanding obstacles of all kinds, including the refusal on the part of the British consul to grant him a certificate as required by the Turkish authorities, he had negotiated and finalized in March 1914 the purchase from Sir John Gray-Hill of Mt. Scopus in Jerusalem, at that time under Turkish rule, with the aim of having a suitable seat for a new university to radiate a new Israeli secular culture. For him there was no religious problem in marrying a Christian, provided they were both nonreligious and provided they agreed to raise a Jewish nonreligious family in Israel. Perhaps he was a bit of a dreamer, but wasn't Israel only a dream at that time?*

He was a man who never hesitated to challenge the views of whatever establishment. On his death in 1933 he presented his priceless library, which included one incunabulum and many very valuable Judaica, to the Pevsner Jewish library of Haifa. (However the incunabulum and all the valuable books never reached their destination.)

I only had a vague notion of the sort of new Israel he had dreamed about, but I knew that his new Israel had to be the beacon for a new culture no longer based on religion, to enlighten the world. So I volunteered and clandestinely went there to share in the fighting for the cre-

---

*Mr. Gideon Shilo, a well-known Israeli researcher, came across my father when researching the outstanding Arab writer and educator Khalil as-Sakakini. He discovered that in February 1914 As-Sakakini had given Arabic lessons to a mysterious Zionist Jew with whom he had interesting conversations about Zionism. To learn Arabic was most unusual among those early Zionists. Subsequently Mr. Shilo wrote an article about his discovery, "The Mysterious Disappearance of 'Hawaja Ibry,'" which was published in *Cathedra,* in December 1990. In this article Mr. Shilo explores the possible reasons for my father's "disappearance from the history of Zionist settlement."

The article mentions my father's purchase in 1914 of the house and the estate of Sir John Gray-Hill on Mt. Scopus in Jerusalem with the object of acquiring a suitable venue for the building of a Hebrew university and reproduces the photograph of the postcard my father sent soon afterward to Ahad Ha'am in London with the announcement. A copy is reproduced in Appendix A at the end of this volume. (The original is kept in the Zionist Archives in Jerusalem.)

The strange thing is (which may help to explain why my father's role is nowhere mentioned) that my father's name is not mentioned in the deed of sale. In the official British archives in Richmond I discovered correspondence between the then–British consul in Jerusalem and the British ambassador in Constantinople as well as the Foreign Office in London. This correspondence shows that, after consulting Constantinople and London, the British Consul refused to issue to my father the certificate required by the Turkish authorities for the sale of property to foreigners.

A copy of one of those letters is reproduced in Appendix B of this book.

ation of the State of Israel. As a scout in the new Israeli army, I went on dangerous missions behind enemy lines, and was ambushed and fired on whenever detected. I am happy I did, even though I realized that the State of Israel was not going to be an outwardly oriented beacon for a new culture, but would express an inwardly oriented culture mirroring the diaspora culture of Eastern European Judaism, where there was no distinction between the Jewish religion and being Jewish.

How sad it was for me to discover that because of my rejection of religion and because my mother was not Jewish, even my comrades did not think of me as a Jew. How sad to discover that the narrowness my father disliked so intensely was actually part and parcel of Jewish upbringing in Israel. I know that there are secular Israeli Jews and even atheist Israeli Jews, but in the Israeli culture, Israeli Jews are not the inhabitants of Israel, descendants from the Hebrews of the Bible, but are the people of the Bible who happen to live in Israel. The Israeli Jew receives his or her identity from the old Jewish religion first, and second from the new Israeli reality.

Of course the Jews could never all live in Israel (even if they all wanted to), which means that Jews living outside Israel accept the identity of the country they live in, and in practice their Judaism is a religion and not a nationality. *I do identify with my Israeli Jewish roots, but I refuse to accept, let alone identify with, the Jewish religion. It sounds like a paradox.*

Throughout my life I have been conditioned by my Jewishness: when I was born a Jew in Israel, when I had to hide it during the war in order to survive, when risking my life in the Israeli army, when people were relating to me either with suspicion or with hostility—and by people I have to include many Jews for whom my humanist worldviews were anathema and a betrayal. And with hindsight I realize that such an attitude toward me on the part of non-Jews as well as of many Jews disgusted me so much that it must have contributed to my emotional hostility toward all religions.

The Meaning of It All

The moment we achieve self-consciousness and are able to project our own image to ourselves, we seek a meaning for our existence, preferably a great meaning. And it is all those great meanings which offer us the opportunity and the justification for wars, cruelty toward our fellow men, and genocides. It seems to me that when we start conceiving great meanings for our existence, we provide a moral cover for our aggressive emotions. The meanings we seek are supposed to outlive us, to carry on our image and our memory forever. Perhaps it is precisely this continuous search for meanings which would defeat our mortality, that motivates us to make the world go round. Yes: wars, cruelty, genocides, but also a continuous endeavor for self-betterment and for immortality.

It had been a hot day and now as the air was cooling down a bit, I felt tired and ready to fall into a reverie. I sat down to look at the newspaper there in front of me . . . and I saw my father! It was him: his grey-white hair, his protruding chin, and his usual bow tie. His face was slightly turned away and he looked pensive and somewhat sad. I went up to him. "Father," I said, "please try to understand me. My life experience has been totally different from yours. How could I accept a God unfairly partial to some over others? How could I believe in a religion which would classify me among the lucky ones blessed by a special covenant with their maker? Father, let me explain. You see, I face the world with some courage because I am not protected or helped by any supernatural entity. And I'd want you by my side, to approve of me."

He had now turned toward me and I shuddered under the impact of his glare. I tried to look directly at his light-blue eyes, but soon I had to lower mine: he was my father, and I had to acknowledge it and give him the respect I owed him.

"David, my son," he started slowly, "you are the one I put all my hopes in. You bear my name, my blood. The blood I received from our ancestors. The blood of millions of persecuted, of slaughtered; the blood of the prophets and of all those who contributed to our unique and unparalleled history of achievements."

"But Father," I butted in, "you have got to admit that there is not a shred of evidence supporting the theologies on which religious dogmas are based. Starting with the greatest and most powerful of all myths: the God myth. Wouldn't you agree, Father, that humans are inclined to construe theoretical structures to make their lives easier? Isn't it obvious, Father, that dividing people under the cover of assumed absolute truths, one creates conflicts and frictions based on superhuman differences?"

"You know, David"—his voice was sad now—"you are trying to convince me that I have wasted all my life! That the heroism and the martyrdom of hundreds of generations were all in vain! No, I was not at all religious, but can't you see that it was religion which preserved the Jewish identity, and so we have to build our new national identity in our country on the strength of the old one? And even when our country is secured, even though we Jews in Israel may do without religion, we will still need the support of the Jews outside who will still rely on religion for their identity. David, I am speaking out of my heart when I warn you that your humanism will never be an identity."

I was taken aback. How could I pit reason and common sense against emotion? Of course he would misunderstand me, because he was so deeply emotionally involved. It was the history of my life which built up my emotional partiality for humanism. And if humanism will not provide me with an identity, I can't lie to myself just for the sake of sharing a religious identity which doesn't make sense to me. But I have to acknowledge that just as my reasoning is strongly influenced by my emotions, obviously my father's life experience had generated emotions different from mine. I love my father, so I have got to find a way. Why hurt him so much?

If emotions are that important for a meaningful life, perhaps humanism should offer appropriate settings for developing them, starting with suitable rituals to celebrate the most significant events in our life and ending with actual rites adopting the format of religious rites, though with a wholly humanist content, where humans would be the standard measure of all things. Ethics, human history, the history of nations and of individuals could make up the core of humanist rituals.

No, I was not trying to deny, let alone devalue the importance of our past heritage. I was only trying to divest the heritage received from our forefathers from our present beliefs and practice.

What is Judaism? Just a national religion without which Jewish people would be left without their national identity? Surely the Jews should be able to live in their own land without having to base their identity on religion! On this fundamental issue we seem to agree. Well then, let me try to build on what we have in common: the shared rejection of the narrowmindedness of so many tenets of our religion. So, I'll ask my father to help me to design a framework of nonreligious rituals which could be meaningful both to him and to me, as well as to *all* human beings. And I was making an effort to express my thoughts to him and find the right words . . . when suddenly I woke up.

Rituals and Support

When my son, Benjamin, went to school at age six, his new mates asked him: What are you, Protestant, Catholic, or Jewish? We were in apartheid-ruled South Africa and the way of life, even for the privileged whites, was to closet themselves in tightly knit religious groups. My son was very handsome, with fair hair, large deep-blue eyes, dark long eyelashes, a straight body with an engaging smile and a gentle nature. I knew he would have been welcome in any of those groups.

"We are humanists," I told him, "but of course when you are a grown-up, you will be able to choose whether to remain a humanist or follow whatever religion."

"I understand," he said then. "So where do we humanists meet on Sunday?"

Well, I thought to myself, life is difficult enough, and it is my duty to help him feel he belongs to some group like the others. There were no overt humanist organizations in South Africa at that time, but I discovered a Unitarian fellowship and used to take him to their service once a month. He seemed to like it. Unitarians have no dogma and are open to theists as well as atheists. Their services are modeled on the framework of the evangelical nonconformist services. I noticed that people enjoyed singing together, listening to the sermon and to the news of the congregation, and even the collection. It appeared that people were coming to the service to perform a ritual more than an act of faith.

I was intrigued by the meaning of ritual in people's lives. When Benjamin was older, it would be something I could discuss in depth and at length with him, much better than with anybody else. Our close relationship would allow me to gradually explore his feelings and his motivations. But Benjamin never did grow older, because there on the Durban road he died with my wife in that fatal accident. I was the driver of that car, but survived.

It appears that rituals are a natural manifestation of interhuman group rapports. If only, if only . . . perhaps a relative, a neighbor, anyone—and I mean anyone—would have knocked at my door with a word, only a word of comfort and sympathy. . . . Beni, my son, I know you are no more, but I wish somebody would have helped me to accept it.

Death

My mother comes from a family which traces its ancestry to the year 961, when Meridano di Crusinallo was awarded the title of Palatine Count by the Holy Roman Emperor Otto I as a reward for capturing Queen Vilma, the widow of Berengario II, and her castle on the island of St. Giulio in Lake Orta. The Crusinallos also produced a pope: Alexander V.

When my mother died, she was cremated in an exclusively secular ritual without any supernatural reference whatsoever. Her family was shocked and could hardly believe it. Some suspected that it had been my doing and not hers; however, her wishes had been clearly documented, leaving no doubt about how and what she wanted.

My mother was a gentle person with a kindly disposition toward humanity. She was not confrontational and disliked arguing, and she earned the respect even of those who had antagonized her. Her life had been difficult, with problems of the kind she had not been prepared to deal with, but she managed to keep her head always erect, even amid adversities, as when she had to cope with exceptional circumstances in order to protect and safeguard our little family, and though she was often wronged, she never lost her inner trust for her fellow human beings. In a world where the winners are those who practice best their selfishness and their greed, while at the same time invoking the blessing of the Almighty over their mean and rapacious pursuits, she never pleaded for any sort of supernatural help. I learned a lot from her. Though often surrounded by sheep and at times by jackals and worms, at her death she showed how to be a lion.

Why the Afterlife?

The phenomenon of death must have produced a dramatic impact on early humans—the end they dreaded!—what they were trying to avoid by all the means at their disposal. So, the need for a social acknowledgment of death must have generated an apposite linguistic utterance on the part of our early ancestors.

For the Hebrews a dead body was acknowledged as *mt* (*met*) מ ת to which corresponds the Persian *mat* and the ancient Egyptian *môt*. The labial sound M seems to have been the first human utterance, just like we notice in babies. But linguistic communication requires the combination of at least two consonants: a labial and a dental (and in fact archaic written languages such as Sumerian, Phoenician, and Hebrew consist of consonants only). The Indo-European *mrt* seems to indicate the same morphological need present in Sanskrit for the Sanskrit semi vowel R between the labial and the dental consonants *mt*. Accordingly we have the Sanskrit *mrtih,* the High Germanic *mord,* the ancient Greek *emorten* (ἔμορτεν), the Old Slavonic *mird,* the Latin *mortuus,* the Welsh *marw* (all referring to dead persons), and the Irish *muirtichenn* (for dead animals). The English *murder,* though from the same derivation, represents a variation of the original meaning.

My hypothesis is that this points to a common prelinguistic origin which later developed into different language and ethnic groups. Furthermore, always in my opinion, the phenomenon of death as experienced by our ancestors should be seen in the context of their lives and of how they experienced themselves.

Our ancestors must have become aware of the great limits of our human capability. As soon as they realized their limits, they started hoping to be able to overcome them and achieve all their wishes and aims. Because humans have the ability to project images of the future, we plan for achieving and obtaining in the future.

So, when life is experienced as unsatisfactory and unfair, *real* justice could be achieved only in the future in another life after death, where we humans would be free of our constraints.

I would postulate that the subsequent linguistic development of the concept of "justice" (truth, right) is etymologically connected with the acknowledgment of somebody's death. In ancient Egyptian the concept of "justice" is *maât,* apparently derived from *môt,* which means "dead." Equally the Hebrew *hmt (emet)* א מ ת, which means "truth" (justice), appears to derive from *met* מ ת, which means "dead." In Indo-European there might well be an etymological connection between the conceptual idea of *merit* (from the Latin *meritum* and the ancient Greek *meiresthai* [μειρεσθαι]—to obtain a share, to share the reward) and the acknowledgment of death.

The problem with the afterlife is that, being outside our human dimension, it would have no future: no hopes to realize in the future. In fact, if in heaven everything were good, good would become meaningless because not contrasted by evil. Our ancestors dreamed of a fairer deal after death, and that made their struggle to survive more bearable. By imagining hopes to be achieved in another life, they gave meaning to their present lives. However, they failed to appreciate that this other life, as it would have no future, would be without anything to look forward to, devoid of the hopes and the dreams from which we draw meaning. Only by accepting the finality of our demise can we face the reality of the world where we have to live and offer meaning to what we really are by being encouraged to make the most of our lives.

I appreciate the emotional need to achieve some "justice." Is there no alternative to an absurd dream of an afterlife? Is injustice inherent to the human condition, or is there anything we could do for a more just life on this earth?

Human Justice

The pharaohs of ancient Egypt claimed that their rule was based on *maât,* which was interpreted and explained as truth and order in the kingdom. The Hebrews ended their prayers with an invocation for the prayer to become true: *hmn* (Amen) אָ מ ן. The aspiration for justice has always been part of the human condition, but perhaps never as much as in the last two centuries, have men and women tried to realize on earth a just social system to live in. The problem is, how do we define justice?

The various theories as to how to achieve social justice on earth could be summarized in two main antagonistic social systems: socialism and capitalism. The main concern of socialist theory is the creation of a just social system eliminating the opportunities for social inequality and exploitation, whereas the main concern of capitalist theory is the best usage of human nature and motivation toward the practical achievement of a society which would produce as much wealth and individual expression as possible. The two ideologies seem incompatible because whereas socialism advocates the social ownership of the means producing wealth to prevent people from benefiting by using other people's labor, capitalism instead maintains that only the private ownership and free competition between private owners will stimulate and prompt society toward achieving efficiency and creating wealth.

As a young man at the end of World War II, I was drawn to socialist ideology. I was also attracted to its antifascist record. Later as a volunteer in the Israeli War of Independence, I realized that any dogmatic theory about justice on earth cannot represent the human condition if it does not build upon ordinary human mental processes. I have to admit that though the logic behind the capitalist system seems to me to make human sense, the ideology of socialism represents, in my opinion, a step forward toward an ideal model for human justice. This may explain the present-day tendency for some sort of compromise between the two. And it is clear to me that the great human dialogue facing us is about the type and the extent of whatever compromise suits best the human world.

Will Humanism Replace Religion?

Yes, *replace* is the key word. So far humanism has been forced to assume a negative role, antagonizing the established religions in order to win for itself the right to exist and operate freely and openly. Having only just achieved this goal in the democracies of the West, after a hard struggle against the established religions, humanism is in a position to aim at taking over the role of religion, which would imply a difficult transition from antagonizing religion to replacing it. To do that humanism will need both to satisfy and fulfill the emotional needs being met at present by the established religions and to take over the compassionate work of religions.

At my mother's secular cremation ceremony, I played a video which I had prepared earlier. Probably this was the first such video funeral service in Italy. Part of the video consisted of an interview where I asked her about her life experience and her feelings about the main events in her life. One question was how, having been exposed to strong Catholic influences in her upbringing and later to Judaism in her adulthood, she came to reject religion en bloc and opt for a humanist approach.

"You know," she said, "it is true that I had been exposed as a child to a very strong Catholic influence on the part of my mother, but in my makeup I have a great sense of balance and almost instinctively I always felt unconvinced by claims of absolute wisdom about right and wrong.

"Your father was not religious. He passionately believed in a new, nonreligious renaissance of the Jewish people in their ancestral land, and I went along with that. Now I am very old and I have seen a lot more than I ever dreamed there was for me to see.

"From what I have seen, I have come to the conclusion that the world would be a much better place without the destructiveness, the arrogance of assumed certainties, the fanaticism, the absurd divisions, and the sheer nonsense of religions, but it also seems to me that the lay world is still far from being able to supply all the positive aspects of religion.

"I am at peace with myself, and it will be for you and for your children and the children of your children to find a way forward."

The Way Forward

It appears that without assumed advanced knowledge of what is going to happen, we would find it very difficult to function, we would go back to our infancy when we were faced with the huge task of building up all our forecasts of what reaction would follow what action.

When I was at the Institute of the Jesuits, in our classroom we sat at twin desks, possibly in order to fit more pupils into the same classroom. Castelbarco was sitting next to me: we were both tall and had to be positioned at the back of the classroom. As we were both concerned about passing our various tests, we developed a practical way of complementary working. I was weak in Latin translations, which I found exceedingly boring, and he was weak in Italian language essays because he could never think of anything to say. So we agreed that he would give me a copy of his Latin translations and I in return would write an Italian essay for him, after I had finished mine. Of course I would do my very best effort writing my own, and as I was not short of ideas, I had no problem concocting another one for him. Well, the end result was that I did improve somewhat my Latin marks and Castelbarco's essays, i.e., mine under his name, always, invariably always, got better marks than my own. In a way, to get good marks though under a different name did not upset me. On the contrary, I found it funny and I felt some pride in Castelbarco's good marks. However, I was obviously prejudged not to be as good at writing Italian essays as Castelbarco: for me it became just one of the many unavoidable facts of life.

If we have to rely on prejudice in order to make sense out of the complex real world facing us, the way forward for humanism may consist in replacing the prejudice of the certain answers revealed to us by religion with a continuous search for new prejudices offering answers which would help us to explain and forecast. To achieve that, I think it would be necessary to teach children that doubt is much more intellectually stimulating and eventually much more productive than the blind acceptance of given knowledge. Insofar as we have to take action, we cannot avoid being influenced by our own prejudices and expectations. This motivates us to seek whatever we can depend on, and life seems more difficult when doubt erodes our decisions to act. How can we resist the temptation to build utopian religious structures on which to model our prejudgments and expectations? Perhaps by being trained to question and then question the answers again.

How We Influence People

We are influenced by interacting with our environment, our family, our role models, our peers, and our society. Religion is probably the most effective way to influence people. Rulers and leaders have always been quick to grasp this and have used or even created religious dogma in order to mold people into a pliable society abiding by the rule of their laws, because religion forges superhuman models which people are trained into following. Humanism would never try to influence people in the same way. On the contrary, humanism encourages people to do away with superhuman models. The models offered by humanism are human: of people who have fought successfully against great odds, against themselves, their limitations, and their circumstances without any supernatural help.

Up to not so long ago people relied on religion for their identity and justified their existence as part of a divinely preordained universal structure of things. The religion of Judaism preserved the Jewish identity in the Diaspora, but the Jews owe to the Christian religion their unimaginably tragic history of persecution and genocide. Only the advent of a secular society offered the Jews the opportunity to break free from the ghettos. Does this mean that without religion, outside the cruel constraints of ghetto life and in a secular society, the Jews will gradually lose their identity?

I practically grew up without a father's role model and perhaps I have been influenced by how I imagined my father to be, by how I imagined his ideals and his aims. My father was a million percent of a Jew. His Jewishness had nothing to do with believing in the religion of Judaism. It was a nationalistic passion, but not an ethnic one, because if it had been ethnic he would not have married an ethnic non-Jew in order to have a family in Israel. His passion led him to devote his life and his money to the Zionist dream. He was not against the Arabs and had Arab friends who came regularly to visit him at home. In fact, he thought that most Palestinian Arabs descended from the mainly Jewish population who were coerced into Islam when the Muslims conquered Israel in the seventh century.

In America and in Israel there are movements and groups of humanists with a Jewish background who celebrate the Jewish festivals with an entirely nonreligious and secular humanistic content. I wish to suggest that in view of the fact that Christianity is an offshoot of Judaism, why should humanists with Jewish as well as Christian background not celebrate together Judeo-Christian festivals with an entirely nonreligious and secular humanistic content?

And what about "Christianity without Religion"? The Christianity of the Sermon on the Mount and the love message of Jesus Christ but *without God, without dogma, and without any sort of supernatural belief,* i.e., a Christianity based on human rather than absolutely valid and immutable values and therefore on the values of humanism which have to depend on the human condition.

Conclusions

Is religion a scourge? To my understanding religion is one of the many products of our human condition. A very dangerous product though, whose impact on people should be well understood before cutting it down to size.

Of course, there is always another side to every coin. Of course the Gospels exercise a huge emotional appeal, of course the Torah touches the heart of every Jew, and of course Doda Lena and my grandmother felt it was their duty to teach me the Truth. *Because religion invests itself with the mission of saving humanity, in the case of Christianity, and of saving the Jewish people in the case of Judaism.*

The Hebrews were the first to produce the concept of a perfect God and a perfect religion. The consequences of the perfect God and the perfect religion of Judaism, Christianity, and Islam are that their dogmas, and their rules could not be altered or argued with. In the case of Judaism religion takes it upon itself to safeguard the ethnic identity of the believers and in this way creates a perfectly true divine nationalism. It is bad enough when nations are taught to believe they are superior; it is even worse when such a belief is validated by a covenant with a perfect God.

In recent times, in traditionally religious countries such as Italy and even Ireland, whenever the faithful have had the opportunity to debate and then express their opinion on tenets which affected their lives, the result was a democratic rejection of those tenets. So, in my opinion, this is the great task for contemporary humanism:

- In a world getting smaller and smaller, to encourage believers in different and often contradictory TRUTHS to meet one another to discuss why each one's TRUTH is more true than the others'.

- To promote debates on the various tenets, rules, and dogmas of the established religions, leading to the development of a critical outlook toward the supernatural.

- To study the impact and the role of religious rituality in order to evaluate the possibility of replacing its religious content with a humanist one.

Religions sought to help people by teaching them the TRUTH. Humanism ought to help people to learn how to use their own heads for value judgments: i.e., applying democracy to our views about our human world.

I hope that this minor contribution will help.

References

Ernout, Alfred, and Antoine Meillet. *Dictionnaire Etymologique de la langue latine*. 3d ed. Klincksieck, 1951.

Rice, Michael. *Egypt's Making*. Routledge, 1990.

Zipf, G. K. *La psychobiologie du language*. Retz C.E.P.I., 1974.

2

Humanist Views

How would Jews who reject Judaism retain a Jewish identity (if they so wish)? The term *identity* means to be the same, what distinguishes from others. Is there a new kind of sameness among Jews who reject Judaism? Perhaps not, but we all share differences when compared with Jews who follow and believe in Judaism.

I asked these questions to five Jewish humanists: Prof. George Klein, a Swedish world-renowned scientist; Claire Rayner, a famous British author and TV and radio personality; Helen Suzman, a South African politician known and admired all over the world; Prof. Adolf Grünbaum, the authoritative and much-esteemed American philosopher; and Geoffrey Elkan, a well-known British clinical psychologist and musician.

Q. What is humanism for you?

CLAIRE RAYNER: For me, humanism is the logical alternative to religious beliefs. We are a sociable species with many built-in drives and needs that in many ways could militate against our sociability if we didn't learn to handle them properly.

For example, anger is a very powerful emotion created sometimes by an outside threat; we have to learn the difference between a genuine outside threat and an ill-perceived threat from another person. And if we can't tell the difference, we might turn on that other person and harm them or even kill them wrongly. The religious answer to this dilemma is to come up with a commandment, "Though shalt not kill." The humanist answer is to help an individual to find the logical reasons for his or her behavior and alternative ethical ways of dealing with the emotion that will not cause irreparable damage.

Essentially, for me, the central tenet of humanism is, "Never knowingly hurt a person." And you, too, of course, are a person. In practice, this is extremely difficult to follow, because not only does the individual have to take into account and balance the needs of a great many people during the course of each working day and each lifetime, but also the needs of other life forces with which we share this planet. The welfare of the planet as a whole is an essential part of concern about human beings.

GEORGE KLEIN: Regarding the human life as the supreme value and having high respect for human culture.

HELEN SUZMAN: To respect the rights of other people, to uphold the rule of law and due process. To oppose discrimination based on race, color, religion, gender, social origin, sexual orientation, or language.

ADOLF GRÜNBAUM: For me humanism includes atheism but is surely *not confined* to atheism. It includes the broad outlines of an entirely man-centered (*not* male-centered!) ethical code of conduct. Humanists have absolutely no reason to be defensive on this score toward theists: It is patent that the various theistic religions, and the multiple denominations within Christianity (e.g., Roman Catholicism, liberal Protestantism, biblical fundamentalism), clash fundamentally on important ethical injunctions (e.g., the death penalty, divorce, birth control, monogamy vs. polygamy, sexual conduct, etc.) while each of them claims revealed knowledge; it is clear that *they each put into the mouth of God* whatever ethical directives and norms they deem appropriate on other, quite worldly grounds, such as *social control*. That was surely the situation in the case of Moses' Decalogue (the Ten Commandments), the purportedly divine teachings of Jesus, and the Koran, for example. I find it *unintelligible* to be told that Moses literally received the Ten Commandments from God on Mount Sinai, engraved in stone. It won't do to say that such revelation is *taken on faith*, since the assent on faith still requires that one understands the *meaning* of the belief to which one gives assent on faith, whereas the tale about Mount Sinai is largely unintelligible.

GEOFFREY ELKAN: It is a way of life and thought which aims at helping the human race (without neglecting animals and plants) to live happier and more fulfilled lives. It does so by considering the latest developments in science, especially the social sciences, and how they can help us lead lives in which we get on more happily with one another, and help others to do so. Of course it does not accept the idea of some superhuman power with a knowledge of right and wrong, only the powers shown by observation and the sciences (e.g., the power of earthquakes, solar power).

Q. How did you become a humanist?

RAYNER: I didn't know I was a humanist for a very long time, until I happened to come across some material from the British Humanist Association and realized that this was my natural "home." I certainly wasn't brought up to be a humanist.

SUZMAN: By evolution, becoming aware of abrogations of human rights when growing up in a country where race discrimination was the norm and also reaching adulthood during the rise of Nazism and the horror of the Holocaust.

ELKAN: The very first event of my religious, or rather atheist, life? I think I was about seven when I was told the story of the sacrifice of Isaac! I don't know who told it to me, but I can still recall imagining my father, who was not with me at the time, and just *knowing* that he would never have agreed to sacrifice me! No, Abraham should just have refused!

GRÜNBAUM: A native of Cologne, Germany, I was ten years of age when the Nazis came to power in 1933. Shortly afterward, I wondered how a purportedly omnibenevolent and omnipotent God could permit so much evil to exist in the world throughout history, and not just in the form of the ominous Nazi regime. Reading some of the philosopher Arthur Schopenhauer's essays soon disposed me toward atheism. Furthermore, whatever theodicies were known to me then as an answer to the problem of evil, struck me as lame.

Q. Do you believe in God?

RAYNER: No. The reason? It is the same reason which prevents me from believing in Father Christmas, fairies at the bottom of the garden, or beings from outer space sending me messages. The natural order is enough for me; I do not need supernatural ideas.

KLEIN: No. I consider "God" as the ultimate example of wishful thinking. "I am not an agnostic. I am indeed an atheist. My attitude is not based on science but rather on faith. . . . The absence of a creator, the nonexistence of God is my childhood faith, my adult belief, unshakable and holy. My faith is based on my experiences that have convinced me of the power of wishful thinking, our inability and aversion to accept hard facts, our desire to find extenuating circumstances" (*The Atheist and the Holy City*, MIT Press, 1990, p. 203).

SUZMAN: No. I was educated at a Catholic school, and the irrational basis of religious belief there made the whole concept of Christianity unacceptable to me, nor was there any countereducation at home which made Judaism a valuable alternative. What I knew of it seemed equally irrational, full of taboos and religious requirements that I also found unacceptable.

GRÜNBAUM: I have remained a lifelong atheist for two reasons. I do not know of *any* cogent argument for the existence of God, and I think there is telling evidence against it. As to the first reason, I find no merit at all, for example, in recent attempts to invoke the Big Bang cosmogony as a basis for divine creation of the universe: See my "Theological Misinterpretations of Current Physical Cosmology," *Foundation of Physics* 26, no. 4 (April 1996): 523–24.

The intellectual history of the debate on the merits of theism leads me to believe that most of those who *argue* for theism have antecedent psychological motives for wishing theism to be true. That emotional inspiration of man creating God as a figment of his own imagination— as opposed to God creating the world and man—has been treated illuminatingly by Ludwig Feurbach's projection theory, and in Freud's *The Future of an Illusion*, which was largely inspired by it.

ELKAN: I don't. I tend not to believe in things which I do not actually experience, unless I have convincing explanations. I can therefore accept the idea of atoms and of black holes because there appears to be evidence of their existence (and they explain what otherwise could not be explained). Furthermore, the appalling things which occur on Earth would suggest that if there were a god, it (he? she?) is either so impotent or so malevolent that I would have no use for it (him, her). I find this aspect of religion is more like paranoid delusions such as I have met in psychiatric hospitals than like any reasonable way of thought.

Q. You were born Jewish: but do you follow the religious customs of Judaism?

RAYNER: Yes, I was born into a Jewish family (I would argue that no one is *born* Jewish; that is to assume that Jews are a discrete human group, which I doubt, rather than a specific religious grouping, which I accept). Do I follow the religious customs of Judaism? No.

KLEIN: No [I do not follow the religious customs of Judaism]. "It is Sabbath evening and I am the guest of an Orthodox Jewish family. Now for the first time, I realize with some astonishment that these Orthodox Jews are using the same argument as those letters from Sweden: You are religious, but you don't know it.

"I deny it, almost desperately. What kind of God are you talking about? Where was your God while millions were gassed at Auschwitz? . . . Another equally venerable rabbi wrote that Auschwitz was God's punishment of the Jews for secularizing Jerusalem, profaning the sacred language, and establishing a godless state. How can anyone believe in such nonsense? What kind of satanic God would concoct such punishments? Who would want a God like that?" (*The Atheist and the Holy City*, p. 204).

In fact their God is so evil that his only excuse is that he does not exist.

SUZMAN: Yes, I was born Jewish and I do not follow the religious customs of Judaism.

GRÜNBAUM: Certainly not.

Q. If you do not believe or follow the religion of Judaism, do you still consider yourself a Jew?

RAYNER: This is an almost impossible question to answer. I am certainly not Jewish in a religious sense and I am not Jewish in the sense of being part of a discrete special group of humans. But there is a certain cultural input that remains with me and that is unavoidable. Because I grew up for the first eight years of my life in a household that was technically Jewish (though the laws of Judaism were never kept there) and was in regular touch with relations who did keep up the laws of Judaism, inevitably there are rhythms and cadences in my speech, in my thoughts, in my life that derive from that childhood experience. But in the same way there are rhythms and cadences in my life and in my mind that derive from the years from eight and fifteen when, as an evacuee, I attended religious (Church of England usually) school and church services because this suited the convenience of the people on whom I was billeted. So you could say that culturally I have Jewish tendencies. I rather like Bernard's Levin's definition of himself as a "pantry Jew." So you can say that I am, too! I certainly am a dab hand at quite a range of Jewish cooking because my grandmother was, and she taught me.

KLEIN: Yes.

SUZMAN: Yes, certainly. Albeit a secular Jew.

GRÜNBAUM: Yes, indeed. It is a fact of my personal history and identity.

Q. Do others consider you Jewish?

RAYNER: Quite a lot do; especially those who disapprove of my liberal, left-wing, republican, humanist interests and ideas. Certainly, they are the ones who seem to write the most abusive letters along the lines of "Jews like you should be grateful to live here under our lovely queen" and so on. Most of the time I don't know what people consider me; I don't ask them.

KLEIN: Yes, because if they don't, I tell them.

SUZMAN: Yes, certainly. Albeit a secular Jew.

ELKAN: Yes [I consider myself a Jew]. And most people I meet know I am Jewish; some may not at first, but on social occasions it tends to occur at some point in the conversation; among musicians, some know and some do not, depending on how well they know me. Besides, as my wife keeps some Jewish traditions, they may see us lighting candles or they may see our quasi-succah.

GRÜNBAUM: Many of them clearly do.

Q. Is it possible to be Jewish and retain a Jewish identity without believing or following Judaism?

RAYNER: Yes, of course it is. I know a great many people who do precisely that.

KLEIN: I don't know. Probably not. But it cannot be helped, as far as I am concerned.

GRÜNBAUM: As I see it, my Jewish identity is imprinted in my psyche by my personal history and by the way in which I can identify, more or less, with those who were brought up in awareness of the history of the Jews. Such people include native American Jews no less than Jews of European birth like myself, who was born in Germany and lived under the Nazis as a boy. I feel *very sorry* for those of Jewish origin who react with self-hatred to their resentment of the social or career penalties they have paid because of that origin. The fact is that even if I were not comfortable, as I am, with being identified as a Jew, some people in my environment would remind me of it. For example, when I made no bones about my atheism to a graduate course I taught in philosophy, one member of the faculty misreported that I am specifically anti-Christian, rather than generally atheistic.

Let me mention that my wife, Thelma, and my daughter, Barbara, are atheistic Jews in the same sense as I. And my daughter is married to an atheist of Christian origin. But mindful of the risk that even their only half-Jewish twin sons might develop self-hatred, they send them to a Temple (Reform Jewish) Sunday School, where they learn about the history of the Jews and Jewish religious holidays.

Q. Many people believe that all religions (including Judaism) are slowly but inexorably destined to become less and less relevant. How do you believe this will affect Jews in the Diaspora?

RAYNER: It is my guess that this will affect Jewish people around the world, just as it affects all other religious people. But I am not totally convinced that all religions are becoming less and less relevant. We are currently going through a period in which fundamentalism in all religions seems to be growing and becoming even more fiery. I think this is infinitely more threatening to people who profess a religious belief than anything else that is going on. It is threatening:

1. because fundamentalism is a form of mental aberration (*in my opinion*) that does damage the human capacity for wide-ranging thought and intelligent decision making.

2. because fundamentalists of one religion are very likely to attack members of other religions, even to the point of killing them, as we have seen in history; and that could happen again. [And it does. —*Author's note.*]

KLEIN: I cannot tell. I don't know enough about them. It may be quite different between different countries and between different Jewish communities.

SUZMAN: I dispute this assumption. On the contrary, I am alarmed at the increase of fundamentalism in all religions. This can lead to a resurgence of anti-Semitism and adverse effects on Jews everywhere.

ELKAN: Unfortunately there now seems to be a terrible increase in the proportion of fundamentalism/extremists (aided by their absence of birth control). But I think that while at one time the synagogue was used also as a center for Jewish life, it is more difficult for secular Jews to find a means of preserving their identity, and if there really were a decline of religions, they might find less need to retain their identity.

Jews could establish cultural centers, just as artists organize art centers, and we have libraries and concert halls for people who want to read or listen to music respectively. I hate the use of separate schools for Jewish children, which segregate them.

Q. You, I, and all contributors to our book, acknowledge and feel Jewish without believing or following the religion of Judaism. Does this point to a new Jewish identity entirely separate from the religion of Judaism and similar to the identity of other nationalities?

RAYNER: As you will see from my answers to your previous questions, I do not "acknowledge and feel Jewish." *I don't deny my Jewish origins*; I don't deny the cultural links I might have; what I do deny is that I attach any importance to my "Jewish identity." My three children have chosen non-Jewish partners and this gives me no qualms whatsoever. My grandchild is being brought up non-Jewish; this gives me no distress either; and in fact I'm supremely indifferent to the Jewishness or otherwise of anyone I meet, am related to, or am concerned with. In my ideal world, to be perfectly honest, there would not be any national barriers; there would be no religious or political barriers either. Only cultural ones. I would like to see the French culture remaining deeply French, the English culture remaining deeply English, and the Jewish culture also remaining Jewish. But these would be cultures that each human being on the planet could dip into and out of at will for the sheer pleasure of it, just as you dip into and out of dishes at a banquet while actually having one dish in front of you that is your own.

KLEIN: It is hard to know. I would have hoped that secular Israel would shape that type of identity. But it does not look like that. The disastrous elections last May [1998] have increased my greatest fear. It is not the war between Jews and Arabs: we have seen many of those. It is the specter of a civil war among Jews. I hope I am wrong. But with this outlook, I am sure you will understand that I am reluctant to prophesy about the future in relation to your question.

SUZMAN: Yes. Although my adherence to liberal values has always been, and will always be, of greater importance to me than retaining a Jewish identity.

3

Do You Have to Be Religious in Order to Have Moral Principles?

Definitely not!

Hermann Bondi recounts: "As a child I absorbed the very strong ethical attitudes of my parents. Their scrupulous fairness in everything they did, their strong social awareness (stimulated by the poverty of a considerable part of Vienna's population), all these influenced me greatly. But it also made clear to me that religious belief had little connection with moral behavior. . . . My father also mused that it was odd that the most orthodox were often the most shady in their business dealings. [However] out of respect for the traditions, he never charged a rabbi who came for a [medical] consultation, right to the end of his life. . . . Moreover the religion of others was also most unattractive . . . [and] I was unfavorably impressed by both branches of Christianity as well as by the Jewish religion.

"So it became clear to me as a boy in Vienna that ethical behavior had nothing to do with religious belief, [but] I was not aware of humanism nor was I actively looking for like-minded people."

Harold Hillman (see chapter 7) remarks: "Traditionally, religious people have asserted that their systems of morals and ethics were dependent upon their theological beliefs, so that the abandonment of the theology meant abandonment of morals. This correlation is obviously untrue, because, firstly, many religions have carried out, supported, or applauded grossly immoral policies such as the killing of the Canaanites, tortures, the Inquisition, the Crusades, slavery, child labor, etc. Secondly, many nonreligious people have pioneered the moral progress of society; thirdly, nonreligious people share large segments of moral codes, such as the so-called Golden Rule."

*   *   *

Is there any possible connection between wearing the kippa and the tefillin, not lighting any light, not using any form of transport on the Sabbath, and behaving morally? How could intelligent and clever people allow themselves to be mesmerized into the absurd belief that by erecting poles interconnected by wires all around an area, they would be able to behave justly and morally in the circumscribed area (*eruv*) doing what they are not allowed by their religious beliefs to do outside that area?

*   *   *

Geoffrey Elkan replies: "The adherence to some, many, or most (or all?) of the Jewish laws about diet, dress, the Sabbath, I see as mainly the result of childhood conditioning, of the attempts at social cohesion of and social exclusion by a tribe, and—in the case of the Sabbath—as possibly embodying some features which might perhaps actually be enjoyed if allowed rather than forced on people. . . . While many who observe them enjoyed their parents' observance, and some come to do so to gain a sense of solidarity with other Jews, some have gone through a childhood in which they were forced to accept them and have come to enjoy them in a way reminiscent of the mechanism which Anna Freud termed 'identification with the aggressor' in which there is a denial of the original position and often therefore an even more dogmatic acceptance of the new and originally hated position. Shakespeare understood this process when he has Hamlet say of the player Queen: 'the lady doth protest too much, methinks.'"

*   *   *

The confusion or rather the quid pro quo arises from the fact that the rules and regulations "revealed" by Moses to the Hebrews in the Sinai desert did not differentiate between moral rules of behavior and rules about what to eat or not to eat, how to dress or not to dress, what to do or not to do on the Sabbath, etc. The Hebrews were commanded not to kill or steal and, almost in the same breath, to rest and not to light fires on the Sabbath. Such a lack of a theoretical clear-cut distinction between morality and matters which have nothing to do with morality, to my mind, is not acceptable to our modem culture and makes Judaism an obsolete way of life. Perhaps the majority even of religious modern Jews deal with this mishmash of rules by ignoring those rules of Judaism which have no relevance whatsoever to moral behavior. Some non-Jews find such a mishmash an amoral aspect of Judaism and criticize all Jews in general for the minority who obey literally what they assume to be God's will "revealed" to them in the Torah.

As far as dress and food norms, in the free world people are allowed to eat and to dress as they please, provided they don't break the law. However, when it comes to behavior, in our modern secular society the rules of moral behavior are no longer the exclusive realm of religions "revealing" from above how humans should behave. It is up to the members of society to determine by majority rule how they wish to regulate their lives.

But what about compassion, charity, help for the needy, and other unselfish behaviors? Here again there seems to be a lot of confusion between the cultural sources of emotional motivation and the doctrinal sources of religious motivation. George Kelly, in his theory on the Psychology of Personal Constructs, assumes that to come to terms with and make sense out of external reality we interpret it through psychological bipolar constructs such as comfortable/uncomfortable, satisfying/unsatisfying, painful/pleasurable, and so forth.

What do we mean by describing anything as "good" or "bad"? Right at the beginning of Genesis, whoever wrote it described light, etc., as "good," which indicates that the writer was already interpreting external reality through the evaluation goggles of "good/bad." Though "good" or "bad" is obviously a subsequent evaluation of preceding core constructs, by calling what is pleasurable, satisfying, or comfortable "good" we are able to evaluate what reality means to us, what we seek and what we try to avoid. The values "good" and "bad" are self-defined by being complementary; i.e., nothing could be judged as good without its opposite of bad, because if everything were good, this term would lose its present meaning. Accordingly we would also construe behavior as good or bad depending on our evaluation of behavior.

In fact, I believe that from the moment we are born, we have to learn to distinguish what is satisfying and pleasant, which we are going to seek, from what is hurting and uncomfortable, which we'll try to avoid.

I am not implying that our good/bad value judgments are in anyway innate; what I am saying is that, in my opinion, in order to survive we have to interpret reality as either good or bad and consequently apply the learned value judgments to our anticipations of future events, which anticipations will direct our behavior. Because, when anticipating the future and deciding how we are going to behave, we have to rely on images already known to us, somehow elaborated within different contexts, different sequences, and different time dimensions. It follows that when the evaluative element is already present in the known images, what actually happens when anticipating future events may be tentatively described this way:

Images of feeling

Satisfied ——————— vs ————— suffering

when   when

sucking   not sucking

leading to

looking forward

to

feeling sated ——————— vs ————— feeling hungry

This means that we organize our perceptions of reality, i.e., the natural psychological pattern of our mental processes, into a structural framework of good/bad value judgments through which we evaluate first and then behave accordingly. It also means that *it is not religions which prompt us to judge morally. What religions do is simply to fit their particular doctrinal goggles, their specific rules and regulations, onto our natural mental processes which we have developed in order to make sense out of reality.*

And as the mental processes on which we depend for our social value judgments have to be determined by the culture of our society, whatever unselfish and charitable behavior in order to be judged as good behavior requires the cultural sanctioning of a given social culture. So, if good behavior and bad behavior are cultural value judgments we apply to behavior, it means that we have to acquire cultural moral goggles in order to enable us to judge behavior morally. This is why we must look at the Torah and its value judgments in the context of the culture of its time, which was different from the Western culture of our day and age. According to the culture of its time, as in all religions of antiquity, whoever wrote the book of Exodus in the Torah was unable to distinguish, as we do in our Western culture today, between the good evaluation of behavior for following social rules (what we call today moral rules, such as do not kill or steal) and good behavior for following dietary or dressing norms (such as do not eat pork or wear the *kippa,* the Jewish skullcap).

We take this distinction between moral rules of behavior and whatever dietary and dress norms or rules for granted, but it was not so at the time of Exodus. And it is symptomatic that in modern Hebrew, the term from archaic Hebrew used for "ethics" is מ ס ו ר (*masur*), which means that which is forbidden. It was the the Greek philosophers who first started to develop in the sixth and fifth centuries B.C.E. a new lay knowledge of the world based solely on human understanding and human reasoning ability and no longer depending on knowledge revealed from whatever supernatural source.

Accordingly, the Greek philosophers developed a logical human analysis of the various aspects of human behavior which, independently of any religious assessment, would be per se either right or wrong, and they called this branch of philosophy ethics.

Also the Talmud, written in the fourth and third centuries B.C.E., after the return from the Babylonian exile, by developing human dialectical argumentation over moral issues, offers a tentative approach in the same direction.

*   *   *

Adolf Grünbaum points out in his paper *The Poverty of Theistic Morality* (p. 219): "For if God values and enjoins us to do what is desirable in its own right, *then ethical rules do not depend for their validity on divine command and they can be independently adopted.*" But, on the other hand, if conduct is good merely because God decrees it, then we also have the morally insoluble problem of deciding, in a multireligious world, which one of the conflicting purported divine revelations of ethical commands we are to accept. Indeed, Richard Gale sees the thrust of Plato's *Euthyphro* to be the claim that 'Ethical propositions are not of the right categorical sort to be made true by anyone's decision [command], even God's.'"

*   *   *

How can the orthodox justify social value judgments inconsistent with their present culture? They cannot, and therefore one is entitled to judge them as culturally obsolete. Liberal Judaism aims at trying to solve this contradiction. The problem is that either one believes that the Torah is the word of God who must, by definition, be perfectly right in aeternum (in eternity), or that it is instead the word of some humans who could, at the very best, make only a few mistakes.

Only by totally rejecting the religion of Judaism can contemporary Jews hold on to their identity with confidence. Those who adopt the criteria of Judaism for judgments on human behavior, in fact are encouraged to become subjective judges of their own behavior, because rather than trying to understand the actual motives of behavior, they are able to cover it under their faith and strict compliance with the rules and the norms of the TRUTH. To understand, or at least to try to understand, how our mind works is (in my opinion) a necessary prerequisite for the argument against Judaism and all religions. What do we see when we look at behavior through "good" and "bad" goggles? We see what we *feel* is Right and what we *feel* is Wrong. To my mind, judgments of "right" and "wrong" involve our emotions and not only our reason, because what is "wrong" may be perceived as a threat to our well being and perhaps even to our survival, whereas what is "good" may be perceived as rewarding and enhancing. This mental process could be described, as a working hypothesis, with the following dichotomy:

I'd *like* behavior to be *good* vs I'd *not like* it to be *bad*

where *liking* expresses the emotional aspect of the dichotomy: the individual personal emotion of the subject of *liking*. When we apply this dichotomy to our own selves, i.e.:

I'd *like* to be *good* vs I'd *not like* to be *bad*,

we feel the need for being certain about *good* or *bad* and consequently seek the security offered by *certainty*. When we are *certain* of what is *good* or *bad* we name them *right* and *wrong*. Religion offers us *certainty*. How could we fail to approve of what is *certainly right* and disapprove of what is *certainly wrong*? The answer is that doubt leads to progress and tolerance, whereas certainty leads to obscurantism and intolerance (see chapter 5).

*　　*　　*

I put the contents and the message of this chapter to an old friend of mine, Hedy Zucker. Hedy came to the United Kingdom with the "Kindertransport," when children from Austria and Germany were saved by taking them out in the nick of time. Both her parents, though nonbelievers, were later exterminated by the Nazis. "Without being an Orthodox," she told me, "I believe and I just know that God helped me when I prayed to Him before my operation."

What is belief? It seems to me that belief has a strong emotional component, because we rely on some *certainties* to safeguard the integrity of our identity: knowing who we are and being acknowledged accordingly. We feel that without those certainties the whole mental structure on which we depend for coming to terms with reality may be irretrievably destroyed. "And," Hedy added with an afterthought, "why should I doubt what actually helps me in my struggle against the many difficulties of living day to day?"

Albert Ellis, the president of the Albert Ellis Institute for Rational Emotive Behavior Therapy, writes in *Free Inquiry* (Summer 1997):

"Religion is much like bad therapy. Religion helps you feel better because, presumably, God, Jesus, or Allah loves you. Therefore you feel (a) there is a God—which almost certainly there isn't—and that (b) God is on your side, will take care of you, loves you, gives you the right rules to live by, etc.

"Now let's suppose it works. You are depressed and you say: 'I am an alcoholic and I believe in God. God will take the bottle out of my hands.' That works to some degree, but are you really sensible and sane? Religion prevents you from getting the ultimate solution, which is that, despite that fact that the universe has no supernatural meaning whatsoever—there is no God, no fairies, no nymphs—you can still take care of yourself."

Ernest Poser (see his main contribution in chapter 6) very appropriately remarks:

"Religionists invoke an all-knowing, all-powerful God to enforce ethical behavior, much as the law attempts to do in the secular world. Both of these "motivational" systems employ fear, punishment, and reward to encourage the desired behavior by instigating deterrent or corrective measures. The systems differ, in that the law of God is literally 'carved in stone,' whereas common law is designed to vary with places and with times. . . . The new, post-Piagetian view of human development posits that infants, far from ascending a sequence of predetermined 'stages' of maturation, instead form theories about the nature of what they see, feel, and hear. Subsequent input from people, objects, and events leads them to modify their theories in accord with what they think is happening. In that way, ideas about their physical world, but also about the consequences of their actions, the thoughts and feelings of others, in short, the basics of moral awareness are also acquired."

I close this chapter with a contribution by **Howard B. Radest** (whose main contribution is in chapter 8):

"The question posed by this chapter is, of course, a very old one and it has been answered many times in the negative, and not just by humanists. Obviously the answer could be merely self-serving or else reflect the influences on the secularists and the humanists of implicit cultural influences which must include the religious dimensions of culture. No doubt this is part of the story, but only part of it. Above all, since doing ethics is what it is all about—ethics is a 'practical' discipline—it is misleading to make principle—religious or otherwise—the center of moral judgment. This suggests further reflection:

"(a) Unless we go along with Aristotle, it is not necessarily true that 'to know the good' is necessarily 'to do the good.' The claim of moral principle, for those so minded, is only the beginning and not the end of doing ethics. Others approach ethics more empirically and tentatively and not as a deductive discipline. Principles then arise out of experience, evolve and develop, and are not simply brought to experience from some other, nonmoral, source like Moses delivering the Commandments midst the lightning and thunder of an angry and powerful god.

"(b) It is clear on the philosophic record that the derivation of moral principle from religious belief rests on shaky ground. The modern statement is Immanuel Kant's who demonstrates—rather convincingly—that from the same religious axioms, alternative and contradictory moral principles can be deducted. To insist on the connection between religion and moral principle is also to ignore much of the classical Western tradition (e.g., the Stoics) and to admit ignorance of Eastern traditions like Confucianism. Indeed, the *disconnection* between religion and morality has been developed in the religious thought of St. Augustine and John Calvin using the notions of 'original sin' and the 'mysteries of grace.'

"(c) Empirically, it is clear, too, that religious people do not necessarily look like ethical people as in the population of prisons or as in the evident criminal behavior of at least some believers or as in the necessity for forgiveness, atonement, and confession all of which would be unnecessary if religious faith, moral principle, and moral conducts were entwined as cause and effect. Similarly, secularists and humanists do not necessarily look like moral villains, etc. The Kantian insight also turns out to be psychologically and sociologically valid.

"(d) It is also clear, given the plurality of religious traditions and moral principles, that the connection could not simply be put between 'religion' and 'principle,' but rather between this particular 'faith' and that particular 'principle' at some moment in time. But this would force us to an absolute historicism which while fascinating anthropologically, would also evade one of the urgent issues of ethics today, namely the possibility of establishing some basis for moral judgment that transcends social and cultural differences. Without that possibility, the Nuremberg Trials are merely a mask for the vengeance of the victors, the Universal Declaration of Human Rights is a Western imposition on the world and otherwise meaningless, and the broad appeal of democratic rights theory in a multicultural setting is inexplicable."

4

What About "Exclusiveness"?

I was talking to a contributor when this controversial problem of who was and is more exclusive came up. The Christians excluded the Jews from society and forced them to live in segregated ghettos where they were locked in during the night, and out of which the Jews were forbidden to seek work and opportunities to study, earn a living, and socialize.

"But what about the exclusiveness inherent in Judaism?" asked my friend. "Whereas Christianity and Islam seek to convert by hook or by crook as many as possible and have a long, tragic history of entire populations pressured and even forced to convert in order to survive, Judaism is very very strict about offering the opportunity of being Jewish, to the extent of not recognizing conversions effected by non-Orthodox rabbis and now by Israel legislating over which conversion to recognize in order to accept the convert as a Jew. Whereas Christianity and Islam accept the bona fide of persons who state that they believe in Christianity or Islam, thus increasing their number and influence in the world, for Judaism one's beliefs won't help unless he or she has a Jewish mother! It looks as if Judaism tries to exclude the rest from belonging to the chosen people!"

"Let us try," I answered, "to look objectively at these two perspectives. It seems to me that both Christianity and Judaism have worked toward excluding each other throughout the centuries because both Christianity and Judaism are based on the *certainty* of being the repositories of the only real TRUTH, and if you believe that your TRUTH is more true than another truth, you cannot honestly accept as equal and friends those you find objectionable, because not only do they doubt the TRUTH, but in fact they threaten it. Is it not the duty of a believer to protect the real TRUTH from dangers? Look here: I was born a Jew in Israel (according to my birth certificate); I would have perished in the Holocaust if the Germans had caught me; I repeatedly risked my life during the War of Independence as a volunteer in the Israeli army, but for many Jews I am not Jewish and am an illegitimate son because my mother was not a Jew! Do you realize that if I were to die in the land of my birth, according to the present religious rules, I would not be allowed to be buried inside a Jewish cemetery?!"

"This brings us back to Jewishness being identified with the religion of Judaism. Perhaps a new secular state in Israel, *where at present there is no secular marriage*, will one day rectify the absurd exclusiveness inherent in Judaism," remarked my friend.

*   *   *

At the end of October 1997 an extraordinary and historical event took place in Rome under the sponsorship of the Vatican. Catholics and representatives of most Christian churches met in a specially convened symposium to discuss "Two Thousand Years of Anti-Judaism" on the part of Christianity and to reassess the scriptural roots of the two-thousand-year history of Christian enmity and hatred toward Judaism which undoubtedly contributed to so many people either taking part in or accepting the Holocaust.

Christians have been taught by the Gospels, and in particular Matthew, as well as by the Acts of the Apostles and the Letters of Paul, to blame the Jews for having asked the Romans to crucify Jesus. But on the other side the Jews have always sturdily refused to give any consideration whatsoever to the Jewish message of Jesus, later called Christ by the Greek speakers in Hellenistic Antioch.

What was the Jewish message of Jesus Christ? How and why did he want to reform Judaism? He clearly stated that he did not want to change the basic laws of Judaism, but when asked to identify himself Jesus answered time and again that he was a "Son of man." Now we know that he spoke Aramaic and in fact he is reported to have uttered before dying on the cross the beginning of Psalm 22, not in Hebrew but in Aramaic. And in Aramaic "Son of man" means human being (corresponding to the Hebrew "son of Adam"), which term applied to Jews and Gentiles alike. Was this then the message of Jesus Christ? To do away with the exclusiveness inherent in Judaism?

When I put the issue of exclusiveness to **Hermann Bondi,** he commented: "In many religions, the essence of the TRUTH (and how I enjoy your hatred of this concept!) is accessible only to a few (priests, the 'elect', etc.), so the peculiarity of Judaism is that this exclusiveness extends to all Orthodox."

Geoffrey Elkan gets to the heart of the exclusiveness inherent in Judaism by commenting: "Judaism attempts to segregate its members especially from the Gentiles and even from non-Orthodox Jews. This is partly done by insuring that no child of a mother who has not been married in an official way and therefore granted a religious certificate (*ketubah*) is accepted as a Jew. This means that children, particularly in Israel where there is no secular marriage, can be born illegitimate (*mamzer*), punished for the behavior of their parents. How unjust can a religion be, which stigmatizes people for actions they have not themselves committed?"

And **Leonard Sterling,** a retired dental surgeon and a humanist who grew up in a traditional Jewish home ("my paternal grandparents were extremely pious: with my grandfather being a Shamus [Sexton]. My maternal grandmother was also very pious, coming from cantor/rabbinic stock"), offers a synthesis of the traditional Jewish exclusiveness:

"The important characteristics of carrying a Jewish identity are based on faith in one God, piety and belief in the uniqueness of the Jews as the Chosen People. What is the value of piety with no faith and why 'Chosen People' if not unique? *We are Jews; we believe in one God; we eat kosher food and are different from the Gentiles*

(Goyim). Such were the central tenets of my upbringing. This was leavened with emphasis on being chosen by God and being a special people and always I was exhorted to take pride in my Jewishness. Perhaps the emphasis on 'being proud of being Jewish' should be looked at with some suspicion. However, national claims to uniqueness must fall since there is no biological basis for this and certainly modern genetic research has not detected any special form of DNA in Jews.

"As far as Israel is concerned, the paradox of today is that if the Jews of Israel wish to be a light to the peoples of the world, they must give up their ideas of exclusivity and extend the hand of fraternal friendship to the Palestinian people so that all right-minded peoples can rejoice in an unprecedented act of justice and mercy. I know that it cannot be done without risk, but facing a perpetual future with armed vigilance is not entirely safe either.

"The departure of the last anti-Semite will see the passing of the last Diaspora Jew. What will remain will be Israel divided between believing and secular Jews. I cannot see that Jewishness without belief in a God and adherence to religious ceremonial can possibly survive outside of an Israel which ideally will be open to all religions including life stances other than religious ones."

Pearl Joseph is a psychodynamic counselor and group therapist in private practice. Though she was brought up as a Christian, she is technically Jewish (according to Judaic law) by having a Jewish mother. (But according to the thesis of this book, she would be Jewish only if she *feels* an identity with Jewish history and culture.) When she read my announcement in the *Humanist News*, she sent me the following contribution:

"When I first learned of the plan of this book, I knew I wanted to contribute to it. However, I almost instantly doubted that I would be considered 'eligible' for I am a Jew by birth only and still know very little about the Jewish religion. (I was not brought up in the Jewish faith and though I knew that my mother, Sonia, was Jewish, I did not understand the implications of that fact according to Judaism.)

"The question of whether I can hope to be included, selected, or chosen has always been—as I know it is for many people—a thorny one and I have come to think a lot about this most basic of human longings as it relates to the Jewish idea of being 'God's Chosen Race.' Many have already commented on the price to pay for claiming such an exalted position, for it can only invite the hostility and jealousy of those deemed the not-chosen who then feel not only excluded but downgraded, too.

"Those of us who attach any credence to contemporary psychoanalytic ideas regarding rivalry and jealousy know that any adult experience of these emotions always resonates with our earliest and therefore most passionate experiences of them. Every human being, if he or she is to survive our vulnerable infancy, carries as part of his or her developmental baggage, intimations of the paradisiacal time—albeit brief—when he or she experienced himself or herself as central in 'the scheme of things': i.e., mother's or caregiver's close attentiveness to his or her needs. The subsequent loss of this illusion as Sun/Monarch/ Adam is always wounding and sometimes quite traumatically so. A toddler being displaced (dethroned?) by the arrival of a new baby cannot avoid suffering resentment over the loss of a special place plus anxious bewilderment as to his or her apparent failure in giving satisfaction to his or her parent(s) who is perceived as having 'chosen' the rival Darling Baby. The feelings aroused on these occasions— although not always openly expressed—can be of murderous intensity.

"I believe that this was probably so with me. Although I never had a younger sibling to contend with (I was the youngest of three children with a brother of twelve years and a sister of five when I was born), it has always seemed to me that my sister was the 'chosen' and wanted child—especially by my father—while I was unwanted. There was some justification for my view, as my Russian Jewish mother made no secret of the fact and would often repeat the story of how she'd 'fallen' pregnant with me in an unplanned way and late in life. In addition, my birth had nearly killed her and had wrecked her body! In stark contrast to this was the almost fairy-tale account of how the midwife had pronounced: 'This child will prove the Lady of the Family.' (Fate's chosen one?) Meanwhile my 'big' five-year-old sister was firmly established as 'Daddy's girl' plus all the enviable advantages of seniority within our family pecking order. I have always felt very ambivalent over the idea of myself as 'Lady of the family' and have identified closely with the hard-pressed Jew who, so the story goes, cries out to his Maker: 'Lord, I know I am a member of your Chosen Race, but I wish you'd choose someone else for a change!'

"My mother was a great storyteller and never seemed to tire of recounting stories about herself She was the eldest of four and had been her father's favorite and chosen child of whom he'd been very proud, she claimed, particularly over her achievements at school. I can still vividly remember desperately wanting that experience for myself and then feeling 'bad' about it because I knew how short-lived had been Mother's happy times.

"My mother was Russian and her family had fled to England from Brest Litovsk in 1900 when she was ten years old. She could recall the anxiety of that journey with her mother, younger sister, and younger brother—but little else. Her father had preceded them by six months in order to find work and make a home. None of this had proved possible. He had succumbed to TB (rife as it was in those days) and he died within days of their arrival. Fragmentation followed. Her little brother was taken into the Jewish Orphanage, while the mother and the two girls were reluctantly offered 'shelter' by distant and impoverished relatives whom they had never met before.

"By the time my mother, Sonia—a bright child indeed—was twelve, she was her family's breadwinner, working as a sweatshop runner in the East-End rag trade. Her ambition had been to reunite her little family and they now lived in one room just off the Commercial Road. Her doting father had once cherished the hope of a grand education for Sonia, but as things turned out she taught herself to read and write English from discarded newspapers, and although her parents were not practicing Jews she remembered the day when her distraught mother decided to buy the children a slice of forbidden ham in the hope that the pink meat might put roses in their cheeks similar to those of the envied 'foreign' children around them. There were memories too of baitings by those youngsters.

"She was a survivor, my mother, as was my working-class non-Jewish English dad. He was the eighth child in a loving but hard-pressed family. *His* father worked all hours driving a horse-drawn bus. Later, while still in his teens, my dad was to survive the horrors of the

Great War trenches, two injuries, and two years as a POW in Germany. Both my parents were hard acts to follow, as far as I was concerned. I never felt able to achieve anything to match *their* achievements—primarily of dramatic survival and sacrifice. It has taken me over sixty years to recognize that I suffered a form of survivor guilt—that syndrome so familiar to Jews. I think that my syndrome was heightened because my mother was always 'making sacrifices' for her family. She was determined to give us everything she herself had been denied: education, dancing, music, up-market clothes, and toys and treats and holidays. 'I only want you to be happy' was my mother's oft-repeated and reproachful cry.

"I suspect that it was my guilt-ridden sense of failure to bring home the bacon that made me especially vulnerable to stories of Jesus at school. Through assembly-time hymns and prayers and in 'scripture lessons' the Anglican Church informed me that Jesus was God's especially favored son and that 'His goodness faileth never.' Neither of my parents practiced their respective religions, but my mother did talk quite a lot of 'God' to me, it seems. I gained the picture of a huge but invisible 'Him' who watched everything I did—and thought. His disapproval and disappointment couldn't be avoided and the sense of his reproachful 'after all I have done for you' was worse than His wrath. All this awakened me to the first intimations of there being more-to-things-than-meets-the-eye (invaluable to me now as a psychodynamic counselor). This I also understand as more-to-things-than-meets-the-*Conscious*-I.

"At my Church of England school I sang hymns and heard Bible stories, which strengthened the intriguing idea of there being more than one way of understanding things. Before I knew what they were called I learned to love parables. There was also a much-worn morality-tale book at home which supplied, on its back pages, 'The true Meaning' of each story.

"By this time I was also learning something of the Christian attitude to Jews and came to understand that the so-called Chosen Race were regarded as betrayers and murderers of their own longed-for Messiah. It is difficult to be certain how much this affected my personality as I'd never been given to understand that *I* was Jewish. I was to learn this twenty years later—and from my *non*-Jewish husband. *I knew my mother was Jewish, but I never imagined that according to Jewish law, it would make* me *Jewish.* Nevertheless, understanding that I was the child of a Jew perhaps contributed to some extent to the appalling sense of dismay I was to develop in relation to the crucifix. As childhood gave way to the emotional turbulence of adolescence (and against the backdrop of World War II) I found that I couldn't enter a church without crying at the sight of Jesus (whom I loved for his beautiful stories) cruelly nailed to the cross and by the Jews—both his and my own kith and kin. I was an unhappy, perplexed youngster, and this was hard, too, for my parents—especially my mother, who 'couldn't understand why,' who had 'given me everything,' and who furthermore 'only wanted me to be happy.' I couldn't produce the cheerful face she required. I was an ungrateful and lonely lump; an odd-bod with a pretty sister who was not only Daddy's girl but popular with all the boys, too!

"In Scripture-class at school and in church (with the Girl Guides) I heard about 'God's love' and how He would help me if I prayed and believed. I wanted to believe so much and thus belong to God and His *(new)* Chosen and thus 'happy' family—but in this matter too I was a failure. I couldn't believe.

"Thirty years later, at forty-three, I still wanted urgently to believe and to belong, especially as my once successful marriage lay in ruins and my clever husband's mind was disintegrating in presenile dementia. We had very little money and he'd been made redundant, but through the Samaritans I found myself a psychotherapist—and I discovered two books. They were both by John Robinson, late Bishop of Woolwich. His *Honest to God* had created a furor, but it was his *But That I Can't Believe* that really grabbed me. As I read it I felt incredulous. Was this true? Could I trust my eyes? Yes, I could: I *must*. If a bishop (God himself?) was telling me that I could join and *then* be helped to believe because He Himself would help me, then . . . I was saved!

"A year later with much rejoicing I was confirmed into the Anglican Church. Can you believe that I was that foolish? I believe you might. The power of wishful thinking is very great when despair is great. I think most human beings have some experience of gullibility.

"I settled down to learn and listen—to the liturgy, the Readings, the sermons. I began to catch myself doing a kind of Humpty-Dump-tyish simultaneous translation. When I didn't like what I heard, I forced the words to assume a more palatable meaning and one that I could believe. The ugly sister in me insisted, 'It will fit, it will—if I try to pray hard enough.' 'Words mean what I want them to mean!' shouted an inner irate 'toddler.' But I felt guilty doing this. It didn't feel good or honest or make any sense. I was indeed a wretched sinner and for fourteen years I beseeched, 'Lord, help Thou my unbelief.' I never got any further than that prayer. My priest/spiritual advisor said it didn't matter, as God loved me just the same!

"By this time I was endeavoring to do 'God's Will' on several different fronts. Earlier in my life I had a successful enough career as a nurse—primarily in psychiatry, although I'd always felt unhappy about what I'd been required to do. Now economic necessity was forcing me into the role of breadwinner and I felt 'called' to train as a professional counselor. This I was doing *and* working to fund my training and personal therapy *and* trying to hold my husband, our marriage, and home together. My therapy was meanwhile chipping away at my defensive illusions; and then there happened a string of deaths in quick succession. My mother, brother-in-law, husband. . . . There came a morning when, looking in the mirror as I cleaned my teeth I heard my own voice say quite calmly: 'Who do you think you are addressing when you pray? If after these fourteen years you *still* don't believe in the existence of the person you are talking to—well . . . ?' I wriggled and wriggled frantically, struggling to hang on to my disintegrating 'God': (1) My Faith (what faith?) was being tested. (2) I was suffering a massive grief reaction. (3) I was seriously overworking. (4) I finally was crazy and had an auditory hallucination to prove it. (5) God was answering my prayer—but in 'His Own Mysterious Way.' He *was* helping my unbelief—by strengthening it!

"I gave up, sat down and donned my newly acquired psychoanalytic spectacle-frames of understanding and this time for *me*, for all this time I'd been doing a fair job with my clients, believe it or not. Things now began to make some sense. It seemed to me that I had been using my woolly notion of 'God' as something to hold onto—in much the same way as a baby hangs onto a special Teddy, toy, or comfort blanket, and just as the child eventually lets go of its security blanket or teddy bear I was at last letting go of this illusion of security, of the longing to be an acceptable 'little child' in favor of growing up and achieving a measure of fulfillment as a mature human being. I was discovering, too, that there was pleasure to be had in this belated growing up. I no longer depended on *external* approbation to the same extent as previously. I couldn't quite see myself as 'swan' (more of a 'goose,' actually) but I was no longer the (rejected) ugly duckling. Something was happening and there was a lot to be said for it. Something was being born out of my long, laborious reviewing of my thinking regarding God. I no longer feel comfortable using the word, but prefer instead using the concept of a 'something.'

"This 'something' I have come to regard as an attempt on the part of an evolving human conscious mind to deal with, explain, address not only the external world but also a number of elusive though common enough human experiences.

"It is as if the mind confronted with its own bewildering perceptions and productions has reacted by inventing an explanation: the notion of an all-knowing, giantlike, caring parent who has everything most reassuringly in hand and thus understands and deals with everything we cannot. This immensely comforting illusion, which I have come to call Teddy-God, also knows our needs better than we do (again like an effective human parent), but there is a fearful price to pay if we wish to enjoy the protection of this illusory Teddy-God. The price is that we must be 'good' little children. But 'good' defined by whom? 'Good' seems to have come to be understood as a kind of drastically mutilated human being, one without temper, jealousy, dissatisfaction, or curiosity. We must be willing never to defy or explore, to forego the challenge of sexual pleasure, of discovering/learning/tasting the forbidden fruit. Oh yes, challenging and questioning are definitely out! We must expect too to be blamed for our sufferings and difficulties while simultaneously being reminded that we can't possibly attempt to find solutions by ourselves but only by Teddy-God's grace. It would seem that this monstrous teddylike object *of our own creation* advises us that if we will only believe in its existence and the infallibility of its 'wisdom' (so much more wonderfully incomprehensible than our own hard-won experience) and thus disown our bodies and relinquish our minds, then 'all shall be well.' Then there shall be the hugest, bottomless jam-pot (of our own favorite flavor) available tomorrow and hereafter. The rather obvious question as to how we are to enjoy such delights without the means to do so is met with a mixture of stern disapproval and avuncular mystification along the lines of: Wait. All will be revealed! (Of course we won't be around to know if the forthcoming revelation is forthcoming or not—but?) Teddy-God exhorts us: 'Pray to me. Look to me—or else!' (Does that not strike you as a projection of our own narcissism?) The Teddy-God Club echoes this call and then some. They insist they know (based on what?) that a Divine Will exists of its own accord, marvelously similar to ours in some respects yet independent of such inconveniences as human minds and bodies!

"Yes, I am angry, and sometimes that results in urges to smash and hurt because *I* feel smashed and hurt. My illusion has not held up and no Teddy-God comforts *me* as I mourn his passing *and* the loss of so much of my *one-and-only* lifetime spent chasing a mirage.

"It has been a long, hard journey coming to my present way of understanding. There has been so much shame and guilt down the years of my life. My early sense of inadequately recompensing my parents for all they gave me—and tried to give me—was certainly compounded by the discovery that I am Jewish. At that time I understood this to mean kinship with sadistic hypocritical Good Jesus killers, but I also had some sense of pride, i.e., so many brilliant, creative, and funny 'relatives.' I love Jewish food because it reminds me of my mother, and Yiddish humor—ditto. Even now the Jewish (Israeli?) national anthem moves me to tears. It is the first song I remember, and maybe even the only one my mother sang me as a lullaby.

"Confirmation of my Jewishness made sense of the strange affinity I have always felt with many (probably eastern European) Jews. A turn of phrase or familiar intonation; a fleeting gesture; wry shoulder shrug; the witty, perceptive self-deprecation. However, I am also painfully aware that I would have wanted to deny my kinship quickly enough if I'd had to contend with the Nazis. I can't persuade myself that I too would not have been a Judas or a Peter and while there is a value in learning (again) the lesson of humility—it *hurts*.

"Yes, it does *hurt*, this struggle to let go of the longing to be special, whether it is wanting to usurp my mother's or my sister's privileged place in my father affections, wanting to see myself as God's chosen for salvation, or just wanting to like myself a bit more. And so now what? God is dead? No. God was never alive in the first place. However, I *am* alive and, in a way, back where I started, facing the enormity of what it means to be minuscule and sensate in an indifferent universe. However, there is a difference to how it was and how it is. Now I no longer feel intimidated by my Teddy-Minder-God nor compelled to hand over or disown my human attributes. I may be getting old, but I have a fit enough body, good enough mind, and enough aggressive competitiveness and sex drive to give life zest.

"Now that I have learned that I am not the only human being with 'selfish genes' I don't need to protest that it isn't true. It *is* true, and I know that I am driven in a quite ruthless way to fulfill the demands of my genetic programming and social conditioning. I also know that facing this frees a kind of hope in me, for if I can truly own the nastiness which is in me, maybe I need not shrink from facing and tackling other kinds of nastiness and thus begin a degree of remedy.

"Learning such as I have learned has cost me much, but at least I feel more real, less of a fraud. None of it would have been possible without the example of others to learn from and whose own fortitude and commitment has engendered hope in me. Primarily, I cannot imagine how I could have accomplished such as I have without the costly, courageous pioneer work of another Jew—namely Sigmund Freud. It helps too to know that he also had feet of human clay.

"And just what have I accomplished? Well I suppose my biggest discovery is that there is a strange peace in knowing that I am no one special. I can look around me and know that I am not alone. I still mourn the loss of my loved ones, but a sense of them is becoming more established inside me. I mourn too the loss of my Big Illusion and this disillusion makes for a particularly bitter grief nasty for me. Time will help; meanwhile, I don't demand of myself to be cheerful! Strangely my hands feel more open now and able to receive rather than cling or clutch, and it is especially good to receive another human hand now and again in this matter of walking away and pressing on into the unknown region which is both the new and the future—from which no traveler returns."

＊　　＊　　＊

Sidney Epton (see his contribution to chapter 7) sums it up as follows: "I see every Jewish achievement, every Jewish virtue as weakening the cause of the anti-Semites, and I see every example of Jewish sectarianism, 'racial' exclusivity and ordinary wrongdoing as strengthening it."

But I wish to close the chapter on exclusiveness with this contribution by **Jean-Paul Pecker**:

"There is no greater task today than the fight against all racism; than the fight of humanism against all exclusions; than the fight of free, open, and tolerant thought against all dogma. This is what tolerance is about. And it is intolerable that there should continue to be in mature, rational human beings efforts to exclude 'the others' be they women, blacks, Arabs, Jews, Hindus, Tamils, or atheists from living and thinking in freedom."

5

Do Women Matter?

They do, according to the traditional Jewish song "My Yddishe Mama." They don't according to the Halakà (the law of Judaism). Jewish boys, for instance, are taught to pray thanking the Lord for being born male. However, it appears that whereas women are generally more religious than men, this may not be the case in Judaism and in fact a number of humanists born into Orthodox Jewish families started their awakening away from religion under the influence of their mothers. **Hermann Bondi** confirms it in his contribution to this book:

"My mother had a strong dislike of the religion, though she never articulated it as agnosticism or atheism. It was the confining narrowness of male-centeredness that she abhorred. She very strongly objected to women being banished in the synagogue to a gallery (with a grating to stop the men seeing them). She thought it horrid and offensive that a menstruating woman was considered unclean. Though she did not look much beyond the Jewish community, she vastly preferred those of its members who were not Orthodox. She saw to it that I bore the name of her first close relative (an uncle, I believe) to say openly that he did not believe."

Wendy Hillary, describing her "conversion" from an ordinary

Orthodox Jewish woman into a humanist points out that it was the attitude of Orthodox Judaism toward women which led her to question her blind acceptance of its rules and regulations and eventually led her to humanism. Here's her story:

"I was born into an ordinary (whatever *that* means!) Jewish family. My parents, who were both born in Ireland, were from Orthodox Judaism, and they were married in Manchester in the Holy Law Synagogue.

"After I passed my 11+ and went to Southport High School for Girls, I was one of about thirty Jewish girls who had separate prayers taken by one of the older girls. My father died when I was fourteen. At eighteen I married in the Reform Schul which had by then become Southport New Synagogue. I had always sung in the choir and could read Hebrew very well. I learned all the words to songs by heart (I can still sing everything even now).

"When I had my first child, she was 'named' in schul at a Shabbat morning service. When I had my second child—then suddenly I was confronted with having to allow the 'bris' [circumcision]. Oh my! What a terrible thing. A beautiful and perfect male child was to be mutilated by a stranger—an unknown rabbi. How awful I felt—but I accepted it and got on with bringing up my two lovely children.

"I became very interested in voluntary work, and because there was no need for me to have paid work, I became involved in all sorts of things. The Ladies Guild of the synagogue welcomed me with open arms—at last someone with energy and enthusiasm. I became a reliable and committed member.

"The turning point came when we spent twenty minutes (twenty minutes, I swear!) discussing whether there should be red jellies or red jellies and green jellies for the Chanukah party. Suddenly I thought there must be more to life than this for a Jewish woman.

"At this time the Reform Movement had a definite policy of welcoming converts. I quickly became totally disillusioned with this and found that the majority of converts (nearly always women) would have converted to Buddhism or Rastafarianism if that was a requirement. None of them converted as *single* women; they were all to be married to men who were marrying out.

"I began to question what being Jewish meant, and after discussion with many people and much heart-searching we joined the Orthodox synagogue. We were delighted—we felt 'properly' Jewish and more importantly, our children were mixing with 'proper' Jewish children. (How shameful!)

"Again I became deeply immersed in the communal life of the synagogue. I became a teacher in the Cheder (no trousers!), a member of the Chevra Kadisha, secretary of the parents association and of the Jewish Lads Brigade and Jewish Girls Brigade parents committee. I joined the League of Jewish Women and ran a play group in the local hospital, in the children's ward. The hospital asked me to become their organizer of volunteers and I realized that without proper training I had no chance of doing anything at a higher level than as a volunteer.

"I joined the Samaritans and realized that if I could get paid for what I enjoyed doing that would be ideal. I began to question the role of Jewish women and how they were treated by the male establishment who made all the rules and interpreted all the laws, even those pertaining to women. Women were considered good enough to teach Hebrew and religious education (which I did for eight years) to their children but not good enough to speak in synagogue or take full part in services. None of the male members of the congregation were teachers.

"I stood for election to the synagogue council and was voted on, with a substantial vote. (Before then I had represented the synagogue at the board of deputies and became very knowledgeable about Schechita, etc.) However, the antiwomen lobby decided to hold a meeting to 'ratify' my appointment, and I *lost*. I was so cross about this and the smug complacency of the males who ran the synagogue that I decided that I had had enough of the whole Jewish life. I began to question the acceptance I had shown all my life and to think about what I really believed. I knew I just couldn't believe and I argued incessantly with anyone. I became totally anti-Jewish and would not be convinced. Teaching Jewish boys to thank God they hadn't been born women was the epitome of my annoyance; I felt diminished and undervalued.

"Round about this time, my husband and I realized we were growing apart—I just couldn't be the Jewish wife he wanted. I went to adult education classes and got 3 'A' levels, enough to get into university. My husband 'allowed' me to do this (his words) and when I tried to discuss this with my colleagues they all thought I was mad—'Why rock the boat?' was said to me more than once. I had a comfortable existence; why did I want to spoil it?

"In 1977 I was accepted into a three-year social sciences degree program at Lancaster University starting in 1978. I was thrilled—at last I had a place in the world and a status outside the home.

"My husband and I parted in 1979 and eventually, when he wished to remarry, we divorced amicably. (I'm still married to him, presumably, not having received a 'get' [religious divorce].)

"I then became an enquirer and then an attender at a Quaker meeting. The way of life I saw among "Friends" appealed to my sense of fairness and liberty and justice. It was only when I realized (how naive I was) that an acceptance of Christ was needed to fully embrace Quakerism that I left and began an existence where I found I couldn't really believe in anything any more that wasn't 'real.' It became more important to be honest about my beliefs, and to stop the hypocrisy surrounding Jewish life as I had lived it. At last I became an agnostic, questioning everything and not being criticized for it.

"However, I soon found that not having a religion was refreshing, illuminating and liberating. I could live my life how I felt right and no one would criticize me for it. So now, many years on, I have realized that I don't need an unproved existence of something to dictate how to live my life. Just to be without a code to live by except the one that is right for me is far more satisfying than obeying something that has no meaning. I am now a besotted grandma and both my children live their lives in a 'good' way. Neither has any religious faith, but both lead caring lives with warm hearts and are open to new ideas.

"I feel no sense of guilt at my abandonment of Judaism. I do not *ever* deny being Jewish—in fact it's amazing to me how so many people assume that everyone else is Church of England and I'm able to say quite openly and honestly that 'I'm from a non-Christian background.'

"I have found people to be quite accepting of me—as a person. In my job I had to learn a lot about church politics and ecumenical decision making and what all the terms mean. It has been rewarding to discuss it all with people who have a faith, but I find that I do not need to be told *how* to live—my own soul knows better than anyone!

"This is my story of how I came, at last, to humanism. I feel I was always humanist. Reading humanist literature and talking to fellow humanists makes me feel that I've come home. I've started to realize that gut feelings are important and I rely on my instinctive reactions to things. As a result I'm a much happier person knowing that I'm being honest about my views and my upbringing.

"My sister (five years older than me) has not deviated from her religious upbringing. However, she accepts me and my beliefs, although we don't discuss anything spiritual. I feel she leads a life that I am delighted to have escaped from and I know that I have moved away—geographically and philosophically—never to return.

"People who know me and my background say that I react to things in a Jewish way. I know that I feel very strongly about Israel and how Israelis treat Palestinians. I know that Jews feel Israel can do no wrong but oh! I feel they are so misguided. I find the arrogance of Israel difficult to accept although I acknowledge the energy and capabilities shown by people constructing an economy from sand!

"I'm always interested in hearing about people who have gone through a secularization process and how the freedom affects them. For myself, leading a life that feels right for me is the most important thing and not having to live in a hypocritical way is worth everything."

I asked the author and radio personality **Claire Rayner** for her comments on this subject: "One of the things I most dislike about Judaism is its attitude to women, which is both dismissing (the daily prayer thanking God that a male was born with his penis rather than without it) and the patronizing rubbish about women being the 'Queen of the home' which justifies their being shut up in galleries behind their grilles and not being allowed to touch the scrolls of the Torah, *sets my teeth on edge*."

(See also Rayner's contribution to chapter 2.)

Rose Hacker is a giant of a pioneer for women's causes. Her best-seller *The Opposite Sex* was the earliest book "to talk to teenagers." At an age when others might be thinking of retirement, Rose served as a councillor in the Greater London Council. Now ninety-two, she has agreed to contribute some of her thoughts: "There was indeed a sense of opposition," she writes "a feeling that men were [considered] superior. Their word was law. They were pampered and nurtured by their wives. I always resented [the position of] male superiority as exemplified in the synagogue where women sat upstairs in a gallery and looked down on the men playing their part in the ceremonies. I felt particularly jealous of that part of the service where the 'Cohanim' retreated with the 'Levites,' including my father, to wash their hands before blessing the congregation with a particular prayer."

As an example of male domination and its consequences in Judaism, Mrs. Hacker recalls that "when my engagement was announced in the *Jewish Chronicle* in 1930, I received, from an unknown source, a book threatening all kinds of evil consequences if I did not obey Jewish sexual rules about menstruation and the taboo on sex for about two weeks each month. I was informed that menstruating women were unclean, that flowers would wilt at their touch and all kind of terrible things would happen if I did not attend a 'mihkveh' [ritual bath] and be thoroughly ritually cleansed before my husband could touch me."

Derek Wilkes, whose contribution appears in chapter 6, recalls this episode:

"A short time ago a cultural organization appended to a Reform synagogue to which I belong presented us with a talk on 'agunot' or 'chained women' by one of their number. The lady was an able speaker and complained that the 'Halachah,' the body of religious law followed by the Jewish orthodox, makes no provision whatever for a woman to divorce her husband no matter how outrageously she is treated. Even though she can obtain a secular civil divorce by the law of England, she still remains chained to her husband by the laws of the Jewish religion until such time as her husband sees fit to present her with a "get" or religious divorce which he alone can obtain. And there is no machinery to compel the husband to take out a "get." The lady said she had been chained to her womanizing and violent husband for twenty years. And she knew of other "agunot" who had been deserted by their husbands who had failed to pay even the very conservative maintenance ordered by the civil court for their children, and they had had to resort to state benefit as a result. She had had a Jewish boyfriend who, on learning of her status as an 'agunah,' left her, remarking correctly that any child resulting from their union would have the permanent incurable taint of bastardy or 'mamzer.'

"Apparently Jewish Law is quite unalterable because there is no body capable of effecting such an alteration. As many as twenty letters to the chief rabbi, Dr. Jonathan Sacks, had gone completely unanswered and were not even acknowledged.

"I made an impassionate speech in which I said that this law was cruel, stupid and indefensible. At this I was cheered. But I was a little less popular when I said that my heart refused to bleed for this woman because *the chains were entirely of her own making*, She has a simple remedy. Leave the United Synagogue and have nothing further to do with it. How can she give her allegiance to an organization which has rules so vicious and cruel and stupid and which has shown itself to be utterly devoid of compassion?

"The United Synagogue is about as flexible as its offspring, the Catholic Church and Islam.

"I urged the lady to contact the British Humanist Association, which hates cruelty and injustice, and I promised that we would give her a beautiful ceremony when she wished to remarry and that her children would not be tainted. She replied that her background did not allow her *emotionally* to follow my advice and she said she wished to satisfy God who, for some reason, wishes to see her bitterly unhappy.

"I thought of the rabbis in Jerusalem who are making Israel one of the last theocracies. A Jewish woman in Israel cannot marry at all except by following superstitious, religious requirements. I remembered 'Yentl,' the heroine of a short story by that great master singer Isaacs Bashevi. The heroine had a great urge to study Jewish religious literature, but she could not enter an academy because of her sex. So she masqueraded as a boy and studied that way. The Orthodox would not have allowed her to study. They do not grant 'smichas' or religious ordination, or the right to be called in the Synagogue to the reading of the law or hold certain religious offices, to any woman. *If women put up with it, they have only themselves to blame!*"

Dr. Henry Morgentaler is an Auschwitz and Dachau survivor who was brought up in a Jewish secular family in Poland. Both his parents had given up the Jewish religion and become members of the 'Bund,' the Jewish Socialist Party. "It was not an ordinary political party—it was also in many ways a movement of liberation from traditional religion with its acceptance of the status quo. Instead of passive acceptance of persecution, the 'Bund' was promoting the ideas of personal and collective dignity as Jews and calling people to fight for the ideal of a socialist society where Jews and non-Jews would work together to build a just society and where anti-Semitism would disappear. The utopia of a socialist Poland accepting its Yiddish-speaking citizens fully was shattered in the Holocaust." (Both his parents and his sister became victims of the Holocaust.)

Having moved to Canada and while living in Montreal, Dr. Morgentaler joined the Humanist Fellowship of Montreal, became its president, and eventually was instrumental in founding the Humanist Association of Canada (HAC) of which he became the first president. He was chosen "Humanist of the Year" by the HAC in 1973 and by the American humanist Association in 1975. "As a result of my humanist philosophy to apply knowledge and compassion to problems in society," he wrote to me, "I became a proponent of the legalization of abortion in Canada, a goal which after a long struggle I have been able to achieve. I was fighting this battle not as a Jew, but as a humanist. . . . Humanists believe in the equality of women; that they should be given all the opportunities available to men. It is clear that in order to achieve this women have to be freed from slavery to their reproductive function; access to contraception and abortion is therefore essential. The full emancipation of women is a very exciting and promising development and needs to be pursued in all parts of the world. Here again it is the traditional religions that are the biggest obstacles to women's emancipation, and humanists fully support and endorse women's rights."

*　　*　　*

To regulate the relationship between men and women has been one of the first and most important tasks of organized society. For Judaism as well as for Catholicism, the attraction between sexes constitutes a major source of sin and is tolerated only for procreation. Therefore Judaism sets out rules of social customs and behavior intended to safeguard society from the social dangers inherent in the sexual attraction between sexes. Women are considered the objects of men's lust therefore the social rules of Judaism focus on preventing women from tempting men into having sex outside the tolerated aims. *Such views imply a complete disregard for female sexuality.*

The present situation in the Western world is of conflict between the rules of obsolete religious theory and the actual behavior practiced by the majority. Modern women no longer accept the role of passive recipients of male sexual aggression. Modern women actively stimulate and promote male sexuality, following the natural role of many mammals and other species. This natural role is suppressed and suffocated by the behavioral codes imposed from assumed supernatural sources in Judaism and other religions. It is up to humanism to draft new sexual guidelines suitable for the mores of sexual behavior in our day and age, and I hope that humanism will be up to this great task, because humanity is now facing a very serious threat to its survival: overpopulation. Other problems and dangers, such as pollution, would become much easier to solve once the global population starts decreasing. And overpopulation is strictly connected with religious dogmas about sex.

6

On Being a Jewish "Geschmattet"*

Would you believe it? This is how I was referred to time and time and time again by Jews right, left, and center. I did resent it, but then I realized that for my own sake I should try to understand the emotion behind that attitude.

One of the most objectionable features of Judaism is, in my opinion, its claim of a unique and privileged relationship between God and the Jewish people. This claim of being superior by divine design prevents religious Jews from taking off their racial blinkers and looking at the world with equanimity, and it may also explain the natural reluctance of sharing such a privileged position with outsiders. *And how could anyone dare to forfeit such a privileged rapport with God*? Even many "marranos"—Jews who converted after the Counter-Reformation in Spain in order to save themselves, perhaps for fear of losing their privileged position—carried on their attachment to Judaism in secret.

Recalling his youth in Vienna, **Hermann Bondi** writes about Jews who converted to Christianity: "The anti-Semitism in the days of the Hapsburg empire and the Austrian republic was more religiously based

---

*A Jew who converted "out" and is referred to as a worthless piece of cloth.

than the 'racial' absurdity of the Nazis later on. We had some reserve (contempt would be too strong a word) for converts who tried to deny the cultural inheritance of the community they had sprung from."

To convert "out" of Judaism (and become a "geschmattet") is a rational decision, but I think that notwithstanding our assumptions about ourselves, we may not be fully aware of the extent to which our emotions engineer our reasons. If I try to analyze my emotions toward the religion of Judaism, I detect a deep disapproval of this central claim on which Judaism is based: i.e., *the claim of being God-chosen.*

Derek Wilkes, a retired solicitor (Cambridge graduate) and a former opera singer who also served in the Royal Navy, explains how, as a boy, at the root of his reasons for becoming a Jewish humanist, there was his friendship with:

The Boy Next Door

"I was raised in Darlington (county Durham), surrounded by my family, who were largely Orthodox Observant Jews. In fact it probably never occurred to them to believe or disbelieve in Judaism. It was simply part of the furniture. Ever since I can remember, I was forced to attend synagogue and observe the mitzvot [good deeds] and the laws of kashrut [food prepared according to Jewish ritual], all of which I found futile, senseless, and excruciatingly boring.

"My bosom friend was Noel Hair, the boy next door, who was the son of an Anglican vicar and was not forced into the straightjacket I had to wear; but he had to attend church services instead.

"In addition I was forced to attend *cheder,* which I also found senseless and boring. The quality of the teaching was bad almost beyond belief. They taught that I should not believe that Jesus was the Messiah but he was yet to come. My friend next door was taught that he was the Messiah. So he and I agreed that at least one of us was being taught untruths. (Today I realize that we both were.) How strange that we should be taught religion differently when we were taught the same geography and chemistry.

"Later I realized that there were a hundred totally different and mutually contradictory religions in the world and everyone in the world was born with a little religious label tied round his neck and was being forced to learn and believe or pretend to believe the religion of his parents, and that the history of the world and the world's present plight has much to do with the followers of one religion or the followers of one interpretation of that religion trying to force it on the followers of the others, often by murder and torture. Why did it never occur to anyone to institute time and motion research studies to ascertain which prayers were the most effective? I suspect that if this were done there would be no noticeable difference in effectiveness.

"Why was it right for me to fast on Yom Kippur [Day of Atonement] and not for the boy next door? And why was it harmful for my constitution to eat *trief* [food not prepared according to Jewish ritual] though it would not harm the digestion of my friend?

"I remember on one occasion being dragged to synagogue and being deeply moved by the rabbi's description of the terrible suffering of my contemporaries in Nazi Germany. This was in the late thirties. Passionate prayers were said imploring God to relieve their plight. Not only was the Almighty deaf to our pleas, but the ultimate unspeakable horrors of the gas chambers were still only in the womb of time and followed a few years later. I remember my grandfather telling me of his confidence that God would work a miracle as He did when we were slaves in Egypt. Why did He not do so, given his infinite power to change the course of human events? Without the slightest inconvenience to himself he could, in a moment, have thought the SS, the Gestapo, and the concentration camps out of existence, and they would have disappeared in the twinkling of an eye. Why did He not do so? [Did He forget his covenant with the children of Israel? Did He not hear the cries of the mothers, the screams of the children, the groans of the dying? DIDN'T HE?—*Author's note.*]

"I was forced to learn something of the Torah. Much of it I found to be completely absurd, and much of it vicious and wicked nonsense. Why did God kill the Egyptian firstborn? What had the innocent babes in arms done? And what of the mass murder of the Canaanites? And why was the entire human race, except for eight adults, drowned at the time of Noah? Was it not an obscene genocide? I often asked these questions and received only abuse in reply, sometimes with a slap.

"My headmaster was a strong Anglican who was obsessed with hatred of sex in all its manifestations, in justification of which he was always quoting Scriptures. I fear he succeeded in cruelly warping the lives of many of his pupils.

"In my adolescence I was evacuated to the country to escape the bombing. At one stage I was billeted at the house of Christian fundamentalists, who believed and assured me that if I did not believe in Jesus I would be tortured for all eternity after my death. If I did believe in Jesus I would be transported to an everlasting Paradise, even though I had led the life of a villain and only accepted Jesus on my deathbed. But if you are simple-minded and cannot understand about Jesus and sin, you are automatically granted eternal Paradise. So is it not infinitely better to be born a mental defective?

"Then when I was eighteen a rabbi persuaded me to attend a Habonim [left-wing Zionist movement] camp. There for the first time I learned that Israel was being built not by religious Jews but by secularists like myself. For the first time I began to realize the colossal contribution made by Jews in almost every field of human endeavor. But I cannot see that Jewish religious teaching, at any rate since biblical times, has contributed anything at all to human civilization, culture, or welfare. The religious Jews, having originally opposed the Zionist movement, have had a wholly negative effect upon it.

"In my student days, in the course of my making a pass at a young lady, she asked me my religion and I replied that I was a nonbeliever and had none. She rejoined that it was somewhat strange, because I had the appearance and air of a Jewish boy. How extraordinary! How can you look as though you have a religious belief? When on vacation with a group of students, I was asked my religion and I replied 'None,' and it was thought by my fellow Jews, most unjustly, that I was denying my heritage. Does our peoplehood rely only on superstition?

"Who then is a Jew? I agree with the following criterion of Jewishness (formulated at the Brussels convention of secular Jews in 1988), and it is of this and only this that I wish to be a part: "*A Jew is a person of Jewish descent who, over a long period of time, has shown a close identification with Jewish history, culture, civilization, and destiny.* I was and am a Jew: I thought and think to myself that anyone is a Jew who says with sincerity that he is a Jew.

"Many years have gone by and I am more than ever a convinced humanist. I still find it difficult to understand how people believe in superstition and religion. I still find it difficult to understand what God was doing during the many thousand million billion trillion centuries he has been alone before creating the world. Was he reading? Was he thinking? There was nothing to read and to think about. And I still look forward to a world where people are the boy next door to one another."

*   *   *

The "conversion" out of Judaism and the analysis of "geschmattet" humanist Jewishness by **Ernest Poser,** the distinguished and honored professor of psychology and psychiatry from Vancouver, Canada, is of particular interest because he deals with it by recounting his unusual life experience:

"If parental influence, early experience, and peer pressure are the major determinants of religious belief, I was destined to become a free thinker. Though my father was strong on Jewish tradition in the sense of historical awareness, family values, and allegiance to the 'tribe,' he had little use for religious observances, let alone beliefs. In his Jewish secularism he was fully supported by my mother, herself the product of an assimilated German Jewish family hailing from Alsace-Lorraine. Their social circle was shaped primarily by the cultural interests of their friends, regardless of their religious persuasion. Only those professing deeply religious views were regarded, especially by my mother, as coming from a different planet.

"Not surprisingly, my own circle of childhood friends ran the gamut from ultraorthodox Jews to an early member of the Hitler Youth. Not until the latter declared in 1932 that his parents forbade him to continue visiting 'those Jews' did it dawn on me that being Jewish was more than a religious attribute. Soon after, on my first day at the Gymnasium, (secondary school), my future classmates emerged from a huddle with the momentous conclusion: 'Der ist doch ein Jude'

(He must be a· Jew). That was probably the first time I asked myself 'How did they know?' Since we hadn't yet exchanged a single word, they must have picked up on my appearance or perhaps the frightened demeanor of a new boy in the hostile era of the Third Reich.

"Against this background and the refugee years that followed, I became increasingly aware of my Jewish identity. For me, however, being Jewish derived not so much from *feeling* as from *knowing*. I cannot say that I ever *felt* Jewish, but I certainly knew that I was. More importantly, I assumed rightly or wrongly that others perceived me as being Jewish. And this assumption is at the root of my Jewish identity. It is the basis of a kinship I feel with a beleaguered people seen by others as being 'different.' And because being 'different' is historically associated with persecution, it makes some of us loath to be Jewish, but also afraid of denying it, lest we lose the support of our hereditary tribesmen. I use that term advisedly in its wider sense, to mean any group of people believed to be of common stock and acting under a central authority. In the past, that authority could have been a chief or other power figure. Today, the central authority for Jewish tribesmen is the religion of Judaism. [That was certainly the way it was yesterday, but if not yet today I hope that tomorrow a secular Israel will project that central authority.—*Author's note.*]

"One can deny that authority or rebel against it, and that is exactly what I did when, at the age of seventeen, I joined the Rationalist Press Association, which later gave rise to the British Humanist Association.

"Did that make me a non-Jew? Obviously not. What then is left of my Jewishness? Is it the culture, ethnicity, nationality, or all three of these? Never having been a Zionist or particularly drawn to any nationalism of any stripe, I would have to discount nationalism as being my tie to Jewishness. I can see the sociopolitical value of having a Jewish homeland, but deplore the internal religious strife and rigid territoriality that seems to go with it. That leaves culture and ethnicity as possible explanations of that 'pintele yid' still lurking within me. I see these two components as representing Jewish nurture and nature respectively, with all the overlap inherent in that terminology. The culture manifests itself in significant contributions to arts and science but also in Jewish humor, 'gefilte fisch' and the proverbial yearning for learning attributed to Jews. All of these probably have less to do with the religion than the history of the Jews, though some would deny that.

"To assert, as I do, that the essence of being Jewish resides both in its cultural and ethnic components, may be seen as pushing the limits of political correctness. I am certainly not proposing that there is, at this stage in history, anything like a 'Jewish race', but it does seem to me that there is such a thing as a Jewish genotype, i.e., a common genetic makeup accounting for physiological and no doubt psychological similarities among many, though by no means all, Jewish people. [Perhaps a large number of Jews in the West stem from the villages (shtetl) of eastern Europe where Jews interbred for centuries. Worldwide and in Israel it is different.—*Author's note.*]

"Why is this important? Only to the extent that it explains why it makes sense to speak of Jewish, but not of Catholic, Islamic, or Hindu secular humanists. The last three labels refer primarily to religious belief systems and are therefore incompatible with a secular worldview. Only the term Jewish carries both a religious and/or ethno-cultural connotation. . . .

"What attracted me to secular humanism, also known as naturalistic or scientific humanism, was its emphasis on the human rather than the divine or supernatural aspects of life on earth. I could see that my father, who was quite intrigued by humanist literature, stayed away from it as soon as his failing health made him confront his own mortality. That was when I realized that traditional beliefs do not have to be 'true' in order to be comforting. By then, however, I had acquired a scientific education and its attendant impatience with untestable hypotheses. The notion of an all-knowing, all-powerful Creator steering the universe seemed to me unbelievable, quite apart from taking personal responsibility for one's actions.

"Becoming a freethinker was, however, only one of my reasons for joining the secular humanists. I liked their universal worldview, their emphasis on enjoying life here and now, their allegiance to reason, respect for scientific data, and insistence on personal responsibility. Most of all, I found it refreshing to be among people whose zest for inquiry was not hampered by dogmas, superstition, or authoritarian taboos.

"There may have been additional, less lofty reasons propelling me toward humanism. Though I never professed belief in a Jewish or any other God, my parents, relatives, and friends thought of me as 'being Jewish' with all the permanence that attribution implies. Thus 'coming out' as a humanist was quite rightly seen by them as a form of conversion. Many Jews, especially those from eastern Europe, have a word for converted Jews. They call them 'geschmattet,' a 'schmatte' being a worthless piece of cloth.

"Could it be that by converting to humanism I was turning my back on a group I no longer wanted to belong to for fear of incurring further punishment? It is not a comforting thought, but one I must entertain at least as a possible explanation of my early affinity for humanism. Luckily, as is so often the case, the motives leading one to initiate an action are not always the same as those maintaining that action. And I can honestly say that acknowledging my Jewish roots is not a problem for me today, a fact that has certainly not dampened my dedication to secular humanism. Quite on the contrary. I now see it not only as a congenial personal philosophy, but also as a promising approach to conflict resolutions at the personal as well as social and political level. Perhaps the brotherhood of man implicit in humanist thought can accomplish what the Fatherhood of God, touted by most religions, failed to achieve. . . .

"I have identified myself as one who is inescapably Jewish by heritage, secular by conviction, and humanist by choice. What, one might ask, does humanism add to being simply a secular Jew? The answer emerges from the following anecdote.

"My wife is of mixed religious parentage. Her father, though 'geschmattet,' came from a Jewish home; her mother was a benign Protestant. We lived in the province of Quebec, at that time a veritable bastion of Roman Catholicism. There was a Catholic and a Protestant school board. Children of other confessions were classified by exclusion as NRCNP (Non-Roman Catholic, Non-Protestant).

"While expecting our oldest child, we first confronted the vexed question all nonreligious and humanist parents have to face sooner or later: What do we tell our children? Clearly, giving them religious instruction of any kind was not an option, seeing that neither of us was a believer. To identify our children merely as 'secular' would have been honest but insufficient, because declaring oneself to be without religion is no substitute for acquiring ethical conduct and learning about the nature of the universe. Organized humanism helped us to resolve that quandary. Under auspices of a humanist 'Sunday school' (so called only because Sunday was the most convenient day to get together) our children met those of other humanists and together they explored not only the humanist perspective but also the belief systems of their religious classmates. They emerged from that exercise with a clearer understanding of what it means to believe, how important it is to examine one's beliefs, and, if necessary, to change them as new data come to light.

"It has often been noted that in an increasingly secular society such as ours, ethics formerly taught in the context of religion are often discarded when apostates become disenchanted with the sacred doctrine. The challenge for humanists is to show that ethics based on human experience and its consequences can and do exist quite independently from scriptural authority.

"Much of what has been said above may be anathema to adherents of even liberal Judaism. In my view, however, it is totally consistent with being a Jew in the ethno-cultural sense of that elusive term."

7

Awakening from Religion to Reason

Can the Human Search for Knowledge Coexist with Revealed Knowledge?

All peoples have had sets of myths, religious rituals, and superstitious beliefs, but after the Exodus Moses gave the Hebrews a revolutionary set of beliefs based on the superhuman concept of absolute and perfect omnipotence. To be perfect it had to depend on a superhuman perfect source which had to be unique (there could not be two or more perfect omnipotences because by sharing it, their omnipotence would have been curtailed). However, it was a conceptual framework conceived by human minds which had developed the ability to construct new knowledge and new theories different from previous knowledge and theories. Well, there is an old Jewish saying: "You can't have the schora (the goods) and the geld (the money) at the same time!" (You can't have your cake and eat it, too).

When I asked **Hermann Bondi** for a short comment contributing to this chapter, he wrote to me:

"Searching for knowledge is a communal activity and deals with matters that are decidable by agreed methods. As in all human affairs, there is always a provisional air about any result. Statements are valuable if they can turn out to be wrong. Perhaps weather forecasting is a good example. A forecast is valueless if it is so broad and general that it cannot turn out to be wrong. It is useful only if it is so specific that it may be proved wrong. Science has indeed been defined by Popper as consisting of theories that are vulnerable to empirical disproof. We have to live with uncertainty and it is infantile to aim at unshakable assurance. Such a lack of certainty is fundamentally human.

"This is in total contrast with the certainty claimed for their particular 'revelation' by the purveyors of the various religious faiths. Their arrogant claims of a supposedly superhuman (more properly called antihuman) assurance are made absurd by the irreconcilable nature of the contradictory alleged truths of the different religions.

"The only way a true believer in some such firm faith can work together with others trying to extend our (necessarily provisional) human knowledge is by interpreting his articles of faith in so flexible a manner as to rob them of their rigidity. But absolute knowledge is of a wholly different nature from truly human understanding and incompatible with it."

And these are the comments of **Geoffrey Elkan**:

"My views about the possibility of thinking scientifically and at the same time having religious (theistic) beliefs of revealed knowledge have gone through various stages: when young I thought that these two ways of trying to understand the world were irreconcilable, and that a scientist in any field could not hold 'revelationist' religious views; I soon came to meet scientists in the natural sciences who did hold religious views, and I interpreted this as some compensation for a sense of lack of human warmth in their view of their work in the physical sciences.

"Later, when working as a clinical psychologist, I came across the phenomenon of orthodox Jewish psychotherapists, including some who would happily call themselves Freudian or Kleinian. How is this possible? The scientific view does not provide people with any real hope of an afterlife, and no hope of a beneficent extraterrestrial power. So, alongside a rational and scientific way of looking at phenomena—including the phenomena of human behavior—these psychotherapists are very happy to believe in a Jewish God and to follow the 'obsessional' (as Freud termed it) rituals, dietary laws, etc. of the Jewish religion.

"The human mind is extraordinarily capable of relating to different aspects of life in different ways. The existence of people who carry on a normal life in some aspects while harboring paranoid delusions is well known (Freud described such a person, the German judge Daniel Paul Schreber, in volume 12 of the standard edition of his work).

"Attempts to suggest to such believers that they are indulging in wish-fulfilling fantasies are immediately countered with the argument that there is no proof of the nonexistence of God. [But how could one prove the nonexistence of something for which there is no proof that it exists?!—*Author's note*.]

So it now seems to me that many people operate in two different ways at different times: they think and behave rationally at some times, and pray and believe in what are to me psychotic delusions at other times. I write 'psychotic,' but in psychiatry those symptoms which are culturally accepted as 'normal' are not regarded as 'psychotic' nor is the person who has these symptoms diagnosed 'psychotic,' so that strictly speaking I should just refer to them as delusional wish-fulfilling phantasies."

*   *   *

In this chapter I am trying to show the inconsistencies between religious belief and scientific knowledge. Many Jewish scientists, when exposed to the logic of scientific discourse, experience the "crumbling down of the pins and needles" supporting (as in the nursery rhyme about London bridge) their religious beliefs and awake to reason. The problem is that religious belief is based on emotional dynamics rather than rational processes. This would explain why others prefer to resort to acrobatic compromises in order to save the emotional security of their certainties.

Harold Hillman was born into an Orthodox Jewish family. On his father's side the rabbinical line went back to eighteenth-century Germany and probably to eleventh-century France. His parental grandfather was a judge (Dayan) of the Jewish Ecclesiastical Court of London (the Beth Din). On his mother's side ancestors may be traced back to the Vilna Gaon and the Maharal in Prague, the legendary maker of the Golem. He graduated as a medical doctor from the Middlesex Hospital Medical School and embarked on a career in medical research, becoming the reader of Physiology at the University of Surrey and the director of the Unity Laboratory of Applied Neurobiology in Guilford, Surrey. About his "awakening" from Jewish Orthodoxy to humanism, he writes:

"Like other Orthodox children before the Second World War, we went to religious classes four times per week and attended synagogue on Saturdays and the Festivals. On these days we were not allowed to carry anything in our pockets, including money, we were not allowed to go on public transport, to switch on any electrical device or turn on a light. We were also conditioned only to eat the meat of animals killed by ritual (kosher) methods, and we felt sick if we believed that something we had eaten had contained nonkosher ingredients. We learned the Old Testament and the Gemara, and were taught to read biblical Hebrew at an early age. We tried to adhere to as many of the six hundreds and thirteen religious laws as we could, and we regarded fellow Jews as allies in a sometimes hostile world.

"People used to jeer at us when we walked home from the synagogue on Saturdays in our suits. There was little visible anti-Semitism in the shops, radio, or newspapers, but the literary anti-Semitism of H. G. Wells, T. S. Eliot, and G. K. Chesterton was still quite respectable. The treatment of German refugees—known as 'enemy aliens'—in the same way as Nazi sympathizers, was quite reprehensible and never explained or justified, let alone apologized for.

"Although the war was raging, my brother and I each had a bar mitzvah, and read a portion of the Bible in synagogue. The message of initiation into manhood was taken up by me, and was followed by about two years of religious fervor. During this time I actually believed that God listened and responded to prayers.

"At that time I attended meetings of the Left Book Club in a big house in Broadhurst Gardens, near Finchley Road Station, London.

They were well attended and we listened to speakers such as John Lewis, Frederick Mullally, George Orwell, and many others. I became a socialist. As such I found it difficult to believe in the concept of the Jews as a chosen people. The reports of unspeakable atrocities to Jews on the continent of Europe made me ask whether God had *chosen* the Jews for such a fate. Some Orthodox people said that the Holocaust was God's punishment for Jews backsliding, but the views of most Jewish people to whom I posed this question was that it was a trial of the Jews by God, or a mystery. Others retorted that it was a mischievous question.*

"As a scientist, I do not believe that it is logical to be agnostic. Either one believes that there is enough evidence to accept the reality of the existence of God, in which case one believes in him, or there is not enough evidence, and one does not believe in a God. One should not say, 'I will not commit myself,' or 'I do not wish to decide because many other people believe one way or the other.'

"It has always surprised me that an intelligent person can believe that the world was created in six days, that the animals went into the

---

*In "God and the Holocaust," *Free Inquiry* (Winter 1987–88), **Adolf Grünbaum** recalls an article by Lord Immanuel Jacobovitz, at the time Chief Orthodox Rabbi of the United Kingdom and the British Commonwealth, stating in the London *Times* (May 9, 1987) that "The idol of individual assimilation exploded in the very country in which it was invented, to be eventually melted down and incinerated in the crematoria of Auschwitz."

"Now," comments Prof. Grünbaum, "when the S.S.-men who implemented the 'final solution' have their reunions, they can say—on the authority of none other than the Chief Rabbi of the United Kingdom—that they were merely the instrument of the God of Moses. Indeed, if Rabbi Jacobovitz is to be believed, the wrath of God is so indiscriminate that it prompted the Nazis to incinerate devoutly orthodox Jews from all over central Europe, no less than the supposedly wicked reform Jews of Germany. Moreover, the vindictiveness of this God is such that the punishment for doctrinal deviance, even within a Mosaic theistic framework, had to be nothing short of live incineration, rather than some lesser reversible misfortune. Far from being just, a God who indiscriminately assigns wholesale lethal punishment and allows babies to be killed in front of their mothers by S.S.-guards is a sadistic, satanic monster deserving of cosmic loathing rather than worship and love."

Ark two by two, that Elijah went to heaven in a chariot of fire, that a Messiah will come, etc. etc. The explanation which I have is that in the area of religion very clever people, including scientists, can suspend their logical faculties, to become either blind believers or intellectual casuists.

"My conclusions:
- There is no evidence for the existence of God.
- If God were to exist and he were all good, he could not have created evil.
- Of the competing and exclusive religions and gods, only one of the many hundreds could be right.
- Revelations are not communicable.
- The idea that every word and every rule of any scripture was written or inspired by a God is unprovable and simply ridiculous.
- It is understandable that the Jews who described 'their' God, should describe themselves as his 'chosen people.' This is both special pleading and unprovable.
- A religious person must be a casuist.
- Most religions do not obey Kant's 'categorical imperative,' because they are more sympathetic to their own adherents than they are to adherents of other religions, particularly to those of rival or historically unfriendly religions and, naturally, to atheists, heretics, and other nonconformists.
- There is no evidence that prayers work.
- Religions have laid down universal moral principles and ethics many years ago, when economic, political, housing, eating, social, and technological situations were so different from those that pertain today that the earlier codes are now either irrelevant or absurd.
- Those expressing the most upright moral values of their religion have frequently been the most immoral people personally. Even today many world conflicts are fueled by religion.
- With very few exceptions religions have been frightened of, and resistant to, lay education, and the more religious a country was, the more backward it has been, both from a human rights point of view and in technological advancement.
- The Judeo-Christian idea that a generation can be responsible

for the misdemeanors of its predecessors is totally unacceptable. How could anyone be responsible for acts allegedly committed by his or her ancestors long before he or she was born? No court in even the most backward country, except perhaps an ecclesiastical court, could possibly try someone for an alleged crime allegedly committed not by him or her, but by his or her ancestors. This is the sort of logic which the Church has used to hold the whole Jewish people responsible for allegedly inciting the Romans to crucify Jesus Christ two thousand years ago."

Sidney Epton was educated in a grammar school and Merton College Oxford, where he read chemistry achieving an M.A. and M.Sc. (Oxon), and at the Manchester College of Technology (now UMIST) where he carried out research and achieved an M.Sc. (Tech.) (Manc.). This is how he describes his "awakening":

"I know nothing about my father's religious upbringing. At some time in his youth he rejected what he would have called the supernatural basis of Judaism. But he belonged to a synagogue, helped toward the building of a new one when we moved to the outer suburbs, and became a member of its management committee.

"There were valid reasons for his split identity. First, my grandfather lived with us. He observed many of the practices of Judaism such as the daily laying on of tefillim (phylacteries), fasting at Yom Kippur, and abstinence from leavened bread during Passover. My father and mother observed the minimum necessary to keep Grandfather happy and maintain domestic harmony. Second, there was a large Jewish community where we lived. I had to be bar-mitzvahed if my father was to retain credibility in that community. I was sent to Hebrew classes on Sunday morning, learned my portion of the Torah, recited it in the synagogue at the due time. I wasn't allowed to take part in my (state) school's morning assemblies or to attend scripture lessons. Thirdly, in the mid-thirties when the evil anti-Semitic regimes in Germany and elsewhere erupted, overt membership of a synagogue served as a gesture of solidarity against the fascist enemy. As someone has said, religion is more about belonging than about believing.

"The clincher regarding my father's real beliefs was that when I was about fourteen he took me to a lecture series on what was then called rationalism, which we now call humanism. They were organized by the South Place Ethical Society at Conway Hall, Holborn, London. The lectures had a lasting effect on my attitude toward religion. Together with my growing fascination with science, the lectures gave me cause to be skeptical of the biblical accounts of the origin of the universe and life. Eventually they led to my refusal to accept the basic religious beliefs of Judaism, or of any other religion for that matter.

"Never a believer, I do not feel the guilt allegedly suffered, for example, by lapsed Catholics. I am not, as it were, a lapsed Judaist; I am simply a nonbeliever. That situation was reached partly because of my father's closet skepticism and partly because of my scientific mindset and my training as a professional scientist. I knew that as far as the outer world was concerned I was still a Jew. In the days of Mosley and Hitler, one was only too aware of what that meant."

Explaining that the search for knowledge is achieved through scientific activity, Prof. **Evry Schatzman** points out: "A research for knowledge is devoted essentially to scientific research. And scientific research aims at discovering the laws of nature. . . . The main way of doing this work consists in finding the difference between what we observe and what we know . . . [because] observed phenomena are simply due to the effect of processes resulting from the laws of nature."

Now I wish to close also this chapter with some considerations from **Jean-Claude Pecker.** Professor Pecker was brought up as a humanist and rather than describing his "awakening" describes why the theories of the world offered by religions are incompatible with science.

" 'Revealed knowledge' is knowledge 'revealed' to mankind from a superhuman source. It is 'revealed' by intermediaries such as priests or rabbis. They reveal about Moses on the Sinai, or about Jesus in the desert, or Paul on the way to Damascus, or Allah speaking to Muhammad. Accordingly only the 'revelations' of the Gospels, the Bible, the Koran are presumed to offer real knowledge. . . . Earlier on, before these 'revealed knowledges,' there were very naive, often charming, and more clearly symbolic legendary tales: such as in Greek mythology or among the American Indians or in many other mythologies. By developing old myths, obviously inspired by the motion of the moon, sun, stars, or planets; by the succession of seasons; by meteorological phenomena and by the behavior of animals, the symbolism of knowledge 'revealed' by religions can be understood. I am inclined to interpret the knowledge revealed by religions as a sort of sophistication of those old beliefs, old symbols, and old legends. Just like the primitive legends and myths of old, so the 'revealed knowledge' of modern religions should be considered as 'beautiful' symbols, which have nothing to do with truth and reality.

"I am convinced that there is indeed a real world, accessible to my eyes, my ears, or the instruments man can build. The reality of the external world is the only safe basis for scientific knowledge. My brain is part of that world; so is yours; and the brains of all human beings as well as all animals. Even religions are part of the real world, which does in no way mean that religious belief represents a description of reality.

"The only description of the real world we can have is imperfect, just like the shades of Plato's cave. But science is the way to get out of the cave, a safer way than to close our eyes and dream. The scientific logic is based on the old Aristotelian motto σωζειν τα φηνομενα and of a discerning use of what has been ascertained from observing the phenomena. In other words, scientific logic aims at describing in a common language the objective reality of the world. *Real* scientific logic cannot accept 'revealed knowledge,' even on subject matters not, strictly speaking, scientific.

"Having said that, I go back to the meaning of a common language. For us humanists, 'nothing of what is human is foreign.' Our only language is the language of humanity. Our human science, our human logic, our human rules of building scientific knowledge from human observation and experimentation, using mathematics as a tool, is the only language which can be understood in any human tongue. In this sense I strongly feel a humanist; i.e., a modern scientist. Conversely, I do not recognize any validity in a discourse which aims at describing the real world of nature on the basis of some so-called 'revealed knowledge' given to us by a God through intermediaries such as priests and rabbis, or through revelations such as the Gospels and the Bible. All 'revelations' are produced by humans! Whereas scientific knowledge addresses mankind as a whole, using a language common to all humans, revealed knowledge addresses the believers, appealing to their individual emotional perceptions of the world. Therefore there is a fundamental difference between the human continuous search for new knowledge and knowledge which has been given to humans from a source humans are not supposed to argue against. But I am aware that there are people who, for their own appeasement, try to reconcile scientific knowledge with their religious beliefs (at times under duress like Galileo or under painful pragmatic considerations like the present attitude of the Church toward the theory of evolution). *In fact, though, the two points of view have nothing in common: one looks inside toward given knowledge already known, whereas the other looks outside toward discovering new knowledge.* As far as I am concerned, my choice is to look out at the sky, at the world outside as well as at my inner world in a continuous effort to know more."

8

Religion and Identity

If people have to be identified, we need criteria for their identification. In our global culture, group identification is achieved by fitting into a globally acknowledged nationality. Religion (or the lack of it) identifies people within a nationality, but on its own is not sufficient to identify people.

Josh Kutchinsky has pursued journalistic, scientific, acting, and other interests during an eclectic working life. Here is his remarkable contribution.

Am I a Jew?

We cannot own the whole. We are born in uncertainty out of improbability. The tracks of our meandering through time and space are almost completely effaced as soon as we have passed by. This is an intolerable state of affairs. To trap an identity we require a web spun from fiction and archaeological fragments and, as with the spider, the moment the web is damaged or destroyed we set about its reconstruction. Without an identity harsh reality freezes us to the spot. With nothing to push against we move in no direction remaining memory-free trapped in a present without past.

So, are we free to invent anything we like or are there rules to the construction of these webs of identity and personality? I can see no reason for absolute rules—self-evident contradictions such as constructing a tall identity from a short body are allowable, but there is often a price to pay.

And so, in Edgware, a slumbering suburb on the edge of the great metropolis, London, in the middle of this century, I made my first appearance into a world of myth, magic, and memory. I assume there is an evolutionary advantage to the dense fog into which we are all born. For I, like everyone else, can remember nothing of those earliest moments and very little of even my first years. Possibly the advantage is that this blankness allows us to begin the story of our lives as if on the first page of a new book. I wrote myself a tall identity and was fortunate that in the unusually peaceful and ever-prosperous world which I inhabited, traveling through many years I have encountered very few low beams—and those I have, I have managed to duck beneath!

How very different it has been for others born a few years earlier and elsewhere on this globe. All those born in continental Europe were to have their carefully crafted identities shattered by bombs and other engines of war, but some would unknowingly have been labeled at birth (or sometime thereafter) as special targets. Spin an image as they might, no matter how small, the low beams of "Jew," "Gypsy," "homosexual," etc. will swing lower and smack you in the face, extinguishing all hopes of identity as you are pushed blindly forward toward your end.

I am an atheist. God is someone else's poor attempt at fiction. While recognizing the enormity of the forces at play in the universe that shape the destinies of worlds, I do not wish to confine them to such an arbitrary and, to me, unattractive shape. Those who seek comfort in simple tales with beginnings, middles, and ends are often scared of open-ended possibilities. Poor fiction it may be, but I do not, and cannot, deny its impact on the affairs of those who came before. The past provides the threads from which to weave the web with which to trap identity. One strand is surely those naively conceived fabulous creatures that miraculously provide the solutions to all problems—the gods.

Although an inadequate and even undesirable foundation on

which to construct an identity, the notions of gods (including the one and only God) have been inventions, which have provided the catalyst for much creativity—great architecture, music, poetry, and paintings as well as social structures.

And now let me answer the question: "Am I a Jew?" Well, in stereotypical fashion I will answer a question with a question. So, just because I don't believe in God you want me to disown my ancestors, among whom were individuals as great as any of the greatest cathedral builders? The cultural cathedral that is Jewishness is too rich in beauty and too steeped in blood to disown. However, it is merely one of the many threads that I weave to sustain my existence. I find it amusing to imagine my Chinese time-twin born at the instant of my birth in a village in China who, like me, has luckily survived to be alive today. We share so much that it would be terribly sad to deny or diminish all that we have in common by exaggerating our differences: the clothes may be of different colors and sizes but are woven from similar materials and for the same purpose.

*   *   *

Howard Radest is adjunct professor of philosophy at the University of South Carolina–Beaufort. He is dean emeritus of the Humanist Institute, a member of the National Council of Ethical Culture Leaders, a former member of the Board of the Association for Moral Education, and a member of the International Association of Humanist Counselors, Leaders and Educators. In the following outstanding contribution to this volume, Professor Radest describes with great equanimity his journey from the culture of the shtetl (the eastern European village where the religion of Judaism and being Jewish were inseparable) to "indifferentism" and eventually to humanism.

An Affectionate Journey

Like many of my generation in the Brooklyn (one of the boroughs of New York City) of the twenties and thirties, I grew up in a home where

Jewishness was simply the way things were. Our neighbors were Jewish, our schoolmates were Jewish; here and there a teacher might not be, but most of them were: the local shopkeepers (supermarkets didn't exist) we bought things from—the corner grocer, butcher, vegetable and fruit store, and candy store—were Jewish. To be sure this was not the shtetl of eastern Europe but a lower-middle-class city neighborhood. We had paved streets, running water, gas and electricity, indoor plumbing, heating, a good public school, and even a tree or two on the street in front of the small houses, each containing four apartments, that people like us lived in. *Forward*, a Yiddish newspaper, was joined by the *Daily News* or the *Mirror*. *New York Times* and *Herald Tribune* were for other people, and besides they cost three pennies while the *News* and the *Mirror* only cost two. Radio meant music, comedy, and adventure stories like *The Lone Ranger* and *The Shadow* and *The Green Hornet*. But radio also meant broadcasts in Yiddish including the tortures of Yiddish "soap opera." I can vaguely remember listening to *Tsoris Bei Leiten* (*The Troubles People Have*) with my mother and grandmother on Sunday mornings although I don't recall any of the details.

The subway or trolley car—then all of five cents a ride with free transfers—took us to Brighton Beach or Coney Island and, rarely, to Manhattan for an excursion to one or another of the great movie palaces like the Roxy or Radio City Music Hall near Broadway. Of course we noticed, really hardly noticed, churches when we traveled to the beach, but there were none in our neighborhood. They really weren't perceptible to us. The synagogues in our neighborhood were Orthodox in a way—Reform was not "really Jewish" and Conservative did not figure in our vocabulary. Of Queens and Staten Island—two other boroughs of New York—we knew little except the names, and besides that's where the goyim (Gentiles, Christians, others) lived. The Bronx was another country. We were, I suppose, also "orthodox" in a way that it makes any sense. Our food was kosher and we made the usual small contributions to Zionism without asking whether it was secular or religious. It was after all the "promised land" that was at stake and not ideology or politics. Passover and the high holidays were times for getting dressed up and going to shul (the synagogue), but there was little weekly and certainly no daily attendance. I can still recall the smells in the storefront synagogue when we did go—mostly the snuff the old men took but also the age of the congregants and the less than frequent bathing. My mother's parents lived in a neighboring apartment, as did one of her sisters, and they continued a way of life from the "old country." My father's father had died before I was born, but his mother lived within walking distance. His sisters were, I suppose, more liberated. They used makeup, ate pork at the Chinese restaurant but never at home, and surely never talked about it except in whispers. His younger brother, an "actor" on the vaudeville stage, was the family pride and the family shame: pride because he traveled a lot, knew lots of people, always had a good story to tell; shame because he married a fellow performer, a non-Jew and that was a shanda (shame).

I suppose I was about nine or ten when I started to go to Hebrew School. I don't remember the Hebrew name, but it was certainly biblical and began with the words Talmud Torah. It was organized by a man of middle age and despite its grand title met in the dark and windowless basement of his home. He eked out a living teaching a few unwilling kids the aleph-bet (the Hebrew ABC) so they could read, but not necessarily understand or translate, the prayer book. A bit later he would be preparing them for bar mitzvah (confirmation). Of course only boys were expected or allowed to attend.

I was always a pretty good student so, unlike my peers, I developed a genuine interest and with my teacher's encouragement learned to translate Torah from Hebrew into Yiddish and English and a bit later, all of eleven, to read some of the commentaries in the Talmud in the original language. My prize possession, a reward I suppose, was a miniature Torah scroll about eight or nine inches high and with print so small I needed a magnifying glass to make out the words. Yet I was able to find in it the weekly "portion" that would be read on the Sabbath in the synagogue and didn't have to rely on the prayer book. I guess I felt that brought me closer to tradition or something. I heard and then read the stories that grew up around biblical events and figures, a kind of oral folk tradition that embellished the spare language of the Bible stories which only in the last century or so had been put in print and illustrated. There was proud talk at home that I might even become a rabbi.

By the way, theological categories—God, Heaven, Hell, Judgment Day, Messiah, etc.—were never subjects of discussion, let alone debate. Just like Jewishness, God was a presence—more like the air you breathe without noticing—and not really an active and actual personage. At home, the Hebrew prayers were few—like the lighting of candles every Friday night—but then, we didn't expect praying to change things. In the tradition, prayers, after all, were not magic, but appreciation and connection. The only theological reality I can recall was on Passover evenings when a full glass of wine for the Angel of the Lord was left on the table during the Seder. I swore—as did my cousins—that someone had drunk from and half emptied it. A skeptic would conclude that it was only natural evaporation through a long evening in an overheated room, but we would not have believed it if it had occurred to someone to say so. Of course it didn't.

The great change in our lives that I can remember was, inevitably, the result of economic crisis. Of course the country—the world—had been going through a depression but, ironically, our family didn't suffer from it. Instead my father's business apparently did pretty well during the thirties. But just as everything was beginning to turn for others, it was his business that failed. And there we were with rent to pay and food to buy—and no idea where the money would come from. I was young enough—about twelve—not to be allowed to know the details. Parents didn't talk things over with their children then, they just took care of things. But I knew things were going wrong and I worried—but only in the privacy of my own thoughts. . . .

It was getting on to my thirteenth birthday and my bar mitzvah. So the Hebrew lessons began again, and again with a teacher who barely managed to survive on the fees of his reluctant students. My bar mitzvah itself was held at the local Hebrew Home for the Aged, mostly because we could manage to make the small donation it took to use the place rather than the fees the organized synagogues expected. Again, I took it all very seriously and even, along with a few friends, began to attend Saturday religious services. Only now it was in a big yellow-brick building with an ornate temple and a community center and a big budget. The rabbi was articulate, the cantor had a beautiful voice, and there was no smell of snuff or unwashed bodies or the sound of Yiddish. For the first time, there were two different kinds of synagogues within walking distance: one Orthodox, the other Conservative. The family couldn't afford to belong to either but did manage to buy a seat for the high holidays. A few miles away in Lawrence, Long Island, another and much more affluent town, there was a vigorous Reform temple which I heard about but never saw. Reform still wasn't really Jewish. I didn't realize then, but I was meeting class and caste differences for the first time. Brooklyn, after all, had been a pretty homogeneous place. Far Rockaway and the five towns on nearby Long Island were not.

By now I was in high school and while all of our crowd were Jewish, there were a number of Italian Catholics, although we really didn't associate with each other at all. Of course there were no blacks or Native Americans. In this post-bar-mitzvah stage I was even putting on the Tfillen (phylacteries) every morning. I will confess, however, that my sabbath attendance was increasingly motivated by a chance to talk with the girls and, not least of all, to *nosh* some very good food at the *Kiddush* (the Sabbath benediction) after the service, especially when one of the more affluent families were celebrating the bar mitzvah of a son. The rabbi's sermons were often challenging and the music beautiful, but I really think my response to these was essentially intellectual and aesthetic. I was on my way to a typical Jewish indifferentism which rallied to the cause of what later was to become Israel, celebrated the holidays, and simply assumed that Jewishness was a fact of life. In fact, if I had any religious passion at the time it was for politics and not for synagogue. I remember, for example, being active as a teenager in Franklin Roosevelt's fourth electoral campaign. But, in a way, for us, Roosevelt was much closer to active religion than God was.

Strangely, then, for all my ritual practice, I suppose I really didn't take Judaism or religion that seriously and yet I was good at it, enjoyed it, but scarcely paid attention to theological or philosophical issues and certainly not to questions of faith. Changes, however, were on the way. For example, I remember briefly dating a young woman whose parents were, I was told by my friends, very very orthodox and very very rich. That didn't bother me and apparently didn't bother her. We were doing fine. Except that one day I called and was told not to bother calling again. Her father simply wouldn't have it. No explanation given, just a ruling. A bit later, I found out that I wasn't "Jewish enough" for him, which I found a puzzlement. And as with other puzzles, I had to solve it. After all, I went to synagogue—but as it turned out, it was the wrong one, the Conservative one, and besides my family were not and could not afford to be members. And I'd been bar mitzvahed—but without the fanfare and attention of an established congregation. I knew Hebrew and Yiddish and Torah and Talmud. But I wasn't Jewish enough. I was running up against distinctions only partly religious if at all and I was smart enough, I guess, to catch on, but not very quickly. Teenage disappointment isn't all that rare or serious but I think that, paradoxically, Judaism now became part of my self-consciousness and at the same time a move away from Judaism probably can be traced to that event. It wasn't a matter of revelation or of challenging some fanciful and false ideas about the world that did it. Nothing dramatic, just an adolescent experience and what we later came to call an existential dilemma.

Of course, in some way or other I must have been ready for the move from indifferent religiousness to just plain indifference. Gradually, I stopped Sabbath attendance and all the rest. If I hadn't been Jewish enough then, I remember thinking angrily, maybe I wasn't Jewish at all—at least not religiously Jewish, observing Jewish. At the same time, I didn't stay angry for long and even enjoyed the sympathy of my friends, especially the girls. Actually, I had more and more on my plate, so I really didn't think I was missing anything. The sciences, especially biology, fascinated me, and as I neared the college years I discovered philosophy. . . . The first philosophy book I read was Plato's *Republic*. I remember struggling through it all alone as a high school senior and I know I hardly understood what was going on. But it was fascinating nevertheless, a way of thinking that my Torah years and my high school courses had not prepared me for.

All of a sudden there was a world out there that I knew—and yet had never really known—existed. I read the Greeks for the first time, the historians and the playwrights and the philosophers. I touched Christian theology in Augustine and Thomas, found an unfamiliar Judaism in Maimonides and Spinoza. Even the Torah changed as I was introduced to the Book of Job and Ecclesiastes. I even read the Gospels—something my Brooklyn neighborhood would just not have understood. I remained religiously indifferent but was less and less indifferent to what was going on around me. And despite departing Jewish practice, I didn't feel a so-called lack of "identity"; there was enough that was meaningful around me so that I could locate myself without existential angst. In fact I had lots of identities—family and politics and American and student and friend and, yes, Jewish. Above all, ideas fed me, although to this day I hesitate to call myself a "philosopher," it sounds so pretentious. After all, ideas were not "mere" ideas but visceral, real, experienced, and important. And I knew that ideas were more and more the place where I wanted to live.

But ideas had consequences in the world. It was not an effete estheticism that drew me to them at all, not the "ivory tower" of intellectualism. Back then Columbia, especially but not only its philosophy department, was still a center of naturalism and pragmatism. John Dewey, although still alive, was not teaching but was very much a presence. His colleagues and his students were in the classroom and I gratefully learned from them. And it all rubbed off on me and, I am sure, lots of others. Of course, I was still Jewish, too—no other option seemed either necessary or important.

That's how I identified myself to the Jewish chaplain when asked about religious preference and I didn't think to do otherwise. Besides, among my fellow students there were lots of Catholics and Protestants and even a few Muslims and Hindus and they didn't seem at all concerned either with combining beneficent labeling and actual indifference. Not that we didn't care about things. We cared about civil liberties and democratic society, about the "bomb" and militarization, about Stalinism and imperialism. Sure, we worried about career—but we didn't worry all that much because something would surely turn up. And I knew where I was going anyhow—toward a philosophy degree and a university teaching post somewhere, somehow. My parents, of course, wondered at this strange turn and especially how I would earn a living. Philosophy after all wasn't medicine or law or even engineering. But they didn't say too much about it and maybe, just maybe, I'd find my way back to the rabbi that when I was eleven they thought I might become.

Finishing college and earning a degree was not the big event it was supposed to be. In fact, I crept up on it unaware or better, it crept up on me. Having taken some summer courses, I discovered that I had enough credits to graduate a year early and I did. With no little help from Professor Blau, now at Columbia, Louis Hacker, and Felix Kaufman, I was admitted to the New School for Social Research and awarded a small scholarship. And yet another world opened, the world of scholars in exile, of continental philosophy and sociology and psychology. . . .

I suppose the discovery of the time for me—still no religious insight in sight—was the Enlightenment and its critics, the existentialists and the Marxists. My master's essay was a paper on Condorcet but Horace Kallen, a student of William James and my advisor, made me read Karl Marx's dissertation on Democritus, Sartre's *L'Être et le néant*, and take a course on Heidegger with Karl Löwith, one of his students. Suddenly I found myself in the midst of a dialogue where people believed that real things were at stake in the argument. And that was not surprising, for in Europe and Asia and Latin America ideology was not a luxury, not an intellectual toy. Oh yes, ideas counted and not just in bull sessions late at night or in the library. Jewishness, through all of this, simply remained as a background, present but not really attended to nor particularly relevant.

I can still remember a Friday evening in Horace Kallen's study at the New School. It was 1951 and I was moving toward my degree about what came next. Doctoral work, no doubt, but I wasn't sure. Sadly, in America philosophy had been captured by the positivists, the language philosophers, the analysts. It was all very erudite and technical and all so very empty of substance. So the stuff I was interested in, the stuff that had seduced me, the ideas that made a difference were no longer out there in the philosophy departments. Kallen looked up from his massive desk and asked: "How would you like to become a rabbi without portfolio?" I was used to his sometimes puckish humor (after all he'd written a book he called *Secularism Is the Will of God*) so I played along and answered, "That's interesting; what does it mean?" Then he told me of his correspondence with David Muzzey, the Columbia University historian and a leader in the Ethical Culture societies, who had written asking him to suggest candidates for its leadership training program. I remember thinking that this sounded a bit more interesting than teaching freshman logic or playing word games. But I also remember that the little I'd heard about Ethical Culture—admittedly from those who had no use for it—was that it was a way for assimilated Jews to escape their Judaism. And I was pretty sure I didn't want that. But, I figured I had little to lose so I agreed that he could send my name in.

For months I heard nothing and had just about forgotten the matter. Then, on a visit to Columbia, I dropped in on Professor Blau, who surprised me when he said that after Muzzey's recent death he'd been asked to talk with me about Kallen's nomination. A few weeks later, Horace Friess, also of the Columbia philosophy department, dropped me a note saying that he and Blau had conferred and that he wanted to pursue the Ethical Culture career possibility with me. . . . To make a long story short, Friess suggested that my best introduction was to read Felix Adler's *An Ethical Philosophy of Life*. Adler, he explained, who was the founder of the movement in 1876, had also been a professor at Columbia (Friess, in fact, was his son-in-law), and had been the son of a rabbi. I borrowed the copy Friess offered me, took it to my room— by then I was living in a small rented room in the apartment of a friend—and read it through in one night. I think that was one of the very few times that Kantian philosophy stopped me from sleeping.

Looking backward, I can recall that I found Adler's neo-Kantianism interesting but unappealing. But I was struck by his passion for turning ideas into programs and then programs into new ideas— shades of Dewey's reconstructianism, although Adler and Dewey remained intellectual adversaries on the Columbia campus. I was to discover that this Adlerian pragmatism was no mere pose but fact. A long record of moral action in the name of moral ideas served as verification of Adler's passion. There were schools and camps, social agencies and political reform committees, public inquiries into corruption, demands for economic and political change—and all in the name of a religion that deliberately left God and Heaven and Hell and Immortality to the individual conscience, that called instead for a worldly and active common faith, a secular religion, if you will. Perhaps what most struck a particular chord with me, a passage I return to every time I meet a raucous humanist, was Adler's autobiographical comment about his departure from Judaism:

> The separation was not violent . . . there were none of those painful struggles which many others have had to undergo when breaking away from the faith of their fathers . . . I have never felt the bitterness often characteristic of the radical, nor his vengeful impulse to retaliate upon those who had imposed the yoke of dogmas upon his soul. I had never worn the yoke. . . . And consequently the wine did not turn into vinegar, the love into hate. . . . One day I awoke and found that I had traveled into a new country. . . .

I read those words in the spring of 1951. They spoke to me then; they speak to me still. Indeed if one I moment ever can be said to define and redefine my humanist biography, it was that brief paragraph read and reread of an evening. Of course in the nearly fifty years since, vocabularies have changed. We talk the language of humanism more easily than we did then, for example. And the moral and religious scene has changed: it is more difficult to work out "ethics as a religion" in a pluralist world where ethics is filled with ambiguity and dilemma, religion is all too often a mask for power and self-destroying anger, and human dignity is subverted often by those once thought to be its allies. Nor is it as simple as perhaps it once was to ignore ontological issues, to extend intellectual toleration to error, reducing ideas to mere opinion, especially in the face of genetic confirmation of the Darwinian insight and cosmic confirmation of the indefinite extensibility of the universe and especially when the consequences of the untrue are often so deadly. Evil, after all, is not merely the absence of good, not after the Holocaust and Hiroshima.

Naturally I ask myself whether I have indeed traveled into a new country since that moment in 1951 when indifference was replaced by humanism and the Ethical Culture. I have been the leader of an Ethical Culture Society, the director of the American Ethical Union, the dean of the Humanist Institute, the head of the Ethical Culture Field-ston Schools, the cochair of the International Humanist and Ethical Union, and on and on. For nearly fifty years now humanism has been my work, my concern and even, on occasion, my joy.

But is there ever, really, a new country rather than a very old one revisited and reshaped and reconstructed over and over again as the adventure continues. Of course, I see the new in what we humanists are about: the inclusiveness of humanism as against the tribalism of the old; the integrity of humanism as against the autocracy of the old. Yet, where did this new come from if not from those edge-world of the old where the outlanders of the traditions spoke in conscience even against the vengeful and inscrutable gods and their priests. From Judaism to humanism was then not an "exodus" and surely not a con-version, but a transformation—still incomplete. At least, so it was for me. And therefore my departure, such as it was, was and is affec-tionate, even grateful, knowing now even more than I knew then how much of memory and love and idea I carried into the new: so very much of the old reborn into the new.

*   *   *

The evolution from the culture of the shtetl to the melting-pot culture of North America where the immigrant cultures, by acquiring material benefits and much raised standards, were induced to integrate into the ruling Anglo-Saxon American culture, took a large number of North American Jews to "indifferentism" toward the religion of Judaism. But only a few had the guts and the inclination to proceed further with self-analysis and eventual questioning of their mute allegiance to the religious Judaism of the shtetl.

Whereas jumping out of the cauldron into the multinational chal-lenging new world implied following the trend of things, going against the prevailing current in the great North American culture, which is probably the most religious culture in the West, was a completely dif-ferent kettle of fish. Some humanists with a Jewish background became internationalists. **Albert Ellis,** the founder and leader of Rational Emotive Behavior Therapy, recounts:

"I became an atheist when a course in science, which I took when I was in junior high school, informed me that the Old Testament was wrong about the origins of the human race and the 'fact' that it was created by God in seven days. That set me thinking and I gave up my view of the Jews as *God's chosen people* . . . [and] I became a strong antinationalist. As far as I can see, all forms of nationalism are prejudiced—both against internationalists and all varieties of nationalism except their own. This, to me, is arrant one-sidedness and bigotry. I am not saying that nationalism is all bad, for almost all creeds have their advantages as well as disadvantages. Nationalism, especially when rabid, has so many dangers—such as the encouragement of dictatorship, wars, and terrorism—that it most probably does more harm than good.

"Judaism, like most other religions, has a long nationalistic history, even apart from Zionism, which has a worse history. Orthodox Judaism is, like other kinds of fundamentalism, particularly patriarchal and antidemocratic. Reformed Judaism, with which I was raised, is freer and better, but still leaves much to be desired. I prefer to be a citizen of the world, rather than a promulgator of any kind of nationalism, religion in general, and Judaism in particular. No such citizenship as yet exists, but I look forward to its ultimate establishment."

*   *   *

Should the Diaspora Jews Aim at the Internationalist Model?

Obviously we cannot live without a citizenship, without being accepted as members of a community, observing its laws, paying its taxes and enjoying its protection. In the West Jews have no problem with being citizens of their respective countries; however, not so long ago, under Hitler, European Jewry were deprived of their citizenship rights, be they Orthodox or Reform, or internationalists or atheists or *geschmattet* converts! Once deprived of their rights and as they had no other citizenship to protect them, they were fair game at the mercy of the perpetrators of the "final solution."

It seems to me that the good-neighborhood, love-one-another, internationalist model is not at all new. Many religions and in particular Christianity preached it and still preach it. But the way I understand it, the humanist agenda should be, first of all, to understand ourselves well and, having done that, to accept humans for what we really are, so that we can study and make the best of our human condition, rather than, in the footsteps of Christianity, play hypocritical roles. There are millions of "indifferent" Jews in the United States alone. The conventional wisdom is that as long as all those "indifferent" Jews pay lip service to the religion of Judaism, as long as they carry on having their children bar mitzvahed, they will retain their Jewish identity (if they so wish). I disagree.

In my opinion the 'indifferent' Jews, having lost conviction in their religion, find themselves in the fortunate position of being free to ask themselves what Jewishness means to them, and if they want to hold on to it, how to achieve it without faith in the religion of Judaism. *In my opinion, if the Jewish identity in the Diaspora were to rely on the obsolete religion of Judaism for its survival, sooner or later Jewishness would be obsolete.*

Many Jewish humanists feel antagonistic toward Jewish nationalism and Zionism. The way I understand it, nationalism is a natural manifestation of the human condition. It is natural for people to be partial toward kith and kin and to feel attachment to one's own birth marks, but when nationalism relies on religion for its justification and claims an exclusive divine covenant, it becomes very dangerous and provides an insurmountable obstacle to any attempt at equitable dealings among nations.

A God partial to one people, favoring one nation over others, helping his or her chosen side to win battles and wars *is an imperfect God, a God unable to rise above the human natural partiality for one's own kith and kin. Nationalism based on such an imperfect God offers a divine justification to human imperfection.*

Ben Roston is a humanist descendant from an extremely religious great-great-grandfather in Brest Litovsk, Russia, who wrote commentaries to a religious book, Tosefta. In honor of this his family name was changed to "Tesfoye" and his descendants were highly respected and considered a prime Jewish family. On his beliefs he says: "I do not agree with people who are religious, believe in God as an independent power and observe what, in my view, was relevant 2,000 to 3,000 years ago but is well out of date now. . . . While I was quite irreligious, I felt very strongly that I was a Jew. In fact, I could not feel anything else in Poland which in the 1930s was a rabidly anti-Semitic country, so that Jews lived completely separately."

Having come to England to pursue his studies and having discovered new principles for metal detection, he was awarded a Ph.D. for this research. On the creation of Israel he writes:

"I was still overpowered by my strong feelings of Jewishness and the main political issue of concern to me had been 'the Jewish question'— how can we help ourselves and resist attacks by anti-Semites? These were bad enough before the war in Poland but so much more terrible in the Holocaust in which, apart from my parents who luckily visited me in England just before the war, I lost most of my family and friends.

"My feelings were much affected by the creation of the state of Israel. There the Jews at last became similar to other normal nations. They no longer consisted only of middle and professional classes, financiers and tradesmen, but also included people working farms, orchards, and fishing ponds which they had created from deserts and swamps; they had soldiers and armies like other people and all other social classes that other nations had. They were a balanced society, neither better nor worse than others, and, what was most important, they were *normal*. Nothing could have raised my confidence and self-esteem more than this.

"I was thinking of emigrating to Israel and helping in its building. I was very happy there both on this [first] and several other occasions when I visited Israel. I felt at home with people who were my people, who were in charge in their own country instead of having to rely to some extent on the good will of others. However, I was worried about transplanting from life in Britain, where I was already fairly well established, and particularly I feared the influence of religious bodies which seemed very powerful there and might transform the state into a fundamentalist Orthodox community."

9

Conclusions

All nations, all groups of whatever nature, and all families cherish their past history of successes, failures, tragedies, and all events affecting the group or nation. This book is by Jews preaching against the obsolete religion of Judaism. But how could those Jews in the Diaspora who wish to retain a Jewish identity survive as Jews without the religion of Judaism?

Having had the opportunity to relate with a number of humanists with a Jewish background; having read, edited, and compiled many contributions from all over the world, my conclusions are somewhat clearer to me than my original premises. I am now more convinced than ever that the future of the Jewish cultural and historical heritage in the Diaspora resides no longer in the binding force of the obsolete religion of Judaism, but in the role a secular Israel will be able to play by replacing the synagogue with cultural, artistic, sporting, and various other kinds of secular initiatives. As many secular Diaspora Jews do not care about Israel, they might retain a Jewish identity if they replace the rituals of religion with appropriate humanist rituals.

Even before they dispersed into the Diaspora, the Jews were a people bound together by a religion different from the religions of the peoples surrounding them at that time. However, the new Israel of contemporary Jews should (hopefully) develop and evolve in harmony with the progress of our contemporary secular civilization. Of course Judaism will survive for a long time, perhaps longer than other religions. But I hope that Orthodox Judaism will not prevent Israel from projecting a modern secular model role to the Diaspora Jews.

Having said that, I wish to state that this book does not aim at providing answers, let alone solutions. *Exodus to Humanism* puts forward some questions about the dilemma of Jewishness in the modern world and analyzes them in the light of various experiences and opinions of both prominent and ordinary Jews the world over and then *leaves it to the reader to elaborate answers.*

Finally, I would not be too surprised if some rabbis and Orthodox Jews would accuse this book of anti-Semitism. (Don't they say that the greatest anti-Semites were Jews themselves?) In fact I have excluded contributors who see the religion of Judaism practiced in the families they grew up in as "consisting of a mere set of rules about what to eat or not to eat, rules about things to do or not to do, which were all not explained let alone justified from any moral and ethical point of view, but had to be known so that they could be obeyed."*

Jeremy Isaacs, the world-famous producer, writes in the *Jewish Chronicle* (February 27, 1998): "Orthodoxy . . . cannot command the unquestioning allegiance of all. Many Jews will worship in a freer, gentler mode, and still be Jews. Others who do not believe in the God of Moses, or in any other, will not worship at all. Yet they, too, are proud of their Jewishness, and should be encouraged to continue to be so.

"If unquestioning support for Israel fades, as it may, and if religious belief and observance fall, as I believe they will, we shall need another framework to sustain Jewish identity. That framework must, I suggest, be a memory of our past; a knowledge of our history, biblical and postbiblical; a pride in our people's achievements, not excluding—how could it?—Judaism or Israel."

Michael Goldman, a humanist marketing consultant (retired) with MA, MCIM, MBAE, thinks that Jewishness without the religion

---

*Gertrude Roland.

of Judaism will not survive in the Diaspora and wrote about his experience when he tried to celebrate a Jewish festival in a secular way:

"I still feel Jewish, but I doubt whether a feeling of Jewishness can survive several generations of secularism. For a limited time the feeling can subsist on folk memories and on shared cultural elements, such as humor and cookery, just as European immigrants in the USA first maintain and then gradually lose their identities. . . . My Jewish feelings are, I suppose, those of any member of an ethnic minority. This must seem very thin to a religious Jew. I realized some years ago that, from a religious point of view, I could not be a proper Jew. This was when a friend and I decided that we wanted to acknowledge our Jewishness by commemorating Yom Kippur (Day of Atonement) in some secular way. I contacted a hospital to offer our services for the day in some menial capacity, but they politely told me that on Yom Kippur they were short of surgeons, not cleaners. I then contacted some Jewish organization (was it the Board of Deputies?): they said that they would love to have us worship with them. They had totally missed my point, but I then realized how important a part of being Jewish is the religion of Judaism. This experience in no way inclined me to embrace the faith of my forefathers but, to end where these thoughts began, I hope that I would never deny that I am Jewish. I would also hope that this does not entail beliefs which I find it impossible to entertain."

And **Henry Morgentaler,** who led the struggle to legalize women's right to choose abortion in Canada (see his contribution to chapter 5), having stated that "while I never deny being Jewish, I do not believe that my Jewishness should be a barrier to prevent me from fully relating to other people," adds: "Can Jewish identity be preserved without the Jewish religion in a society where Jews are given the full advantage of citizenship without discrimination? I do not know. But I do not believe that Jews should not intermingle with others, or fail to contribute to the societies in which they live."

*   *   *

*In our multicultural globe, I think that the real issue consists in how
each individual feels about his or her identity.*

* * *

Harold Hillman writes: "Despite its negative aspects, in my opinion,
it is important to recognize that in many societies religion binds people
together, because most of the members are adherents of the same religion. In so far as religion celebrates birth, adulthood and rituals, ceremonies and festivals which have deep cultural and historical roots but
do not celebrate killing or persecution of other people, it is a useful
contribution to the life of a community.

"In addition to having a religion, being Jewish is also having a historical memory. It is reasonable to hope that many Jewish people who
are rationalists will continue to remember and learn from the past. *The
Jewish history of persecution and the horror of the Holocaust will
have to be passed on to future generations of mankind.*

"Furthermore I hope that the great cultural tradition of learning,
storytelling, Yiddish writing, Ladino messianism, and humor will continue to enrich humanity. One can be completely rational and wish to
preserve these historical treasures in the same way as we admire
Dante's *Inferno*, Handel's *Messiah*, Gounod's *Ave Maria*, St. Peter's
in Rome, the Dome of the Rock in Jerusalem, or St. Paul's Cathedral
in London, without sharing the religious beliefs which inspired them.

"For the same reason, it would be a great shame if the traditions of
Rosh Hashana, Yom Kippur, Passover, etc., disappeared—not because
they are occasions upon which Jews pray in commune with God, but
because they are very long-established traditional events; sometimes
they are based on history, sometimes on beliefs, but if they disappeared it would be a loss to civilization, like the burning of the Library
at Alexandria, the disappearance of the dodo, or the destruction of the
synagogues on Kristallnacht.

"Thus we may be fascinated by the reflections on human nature
from religion throughout the ages—as was Jung; we may be interested
in them as illustrations of the cavalcade of life and as our own historical heritage. *Nevertheless we abjure the theology of Judaism and*

regard its dogma and 613 rules as irrational and out of date. In addition to rejecting Judaism, we apply the same criteria to all other religions. We do not wish to be tribal, and favor one system of dogma over another."

Leonard Sterling (contributing also to chapter 4) makes a very good point: "Short of the destruction of all written history, the 'Washing away' of Jewishness could not happen. Among the greatest achievements of the Jews, I would put their intellectual honesty and moral courage in resisting the claims of Christianity. As a people without a country they were in continual extreme danger, yet held fast. While the religious life is impossible for me, there will always be those for whom the prospect of life without religion would be equally impossible. In our variety lies our humanity."

*   *   *

After discussing this book, a friend of mine, Rachel Lissauer, commented: "You see, Judaism is not just a matter of belief. Religion with its festivals, its ritual get-togethers at preset dates, its symbolism anchored in history, is a major factor holding families and communities together. I have grandchildren who would be left out of touch by their atheist parents if it were not for me organizing family reunions for the Jewish festivals."

*   *   *

The point appears to be again and again that *we are emotional beings trying very hard to convince ourselves that we are rational beings.* In which case I felt that the best way to close this book would be to ask **Arnold Wesker,** the well-known playwright, to answer some questions on his fascinating theory about the two roots of Judaism, which he has incorporated in the body of his contribution.

The Pains, Pleasures, and
Responsibilities of Inventing God

I have elsewhere argued that there are probably two roots of Judaism. Many Jews, not only artists and intellectuals but artisans and businessmen, claim a profound sense of Jewishness unsupported either by a substantial knowledge of Jewish culture or by religious faith. Impossible! cry the orthodox. Adherence to the prescribed rituals and laws of the Torah is what has kept the race alive and given it its identity. Only those who observe the rituals and have faith in the thirteen principles of Maimonides, and of course only those who descend from Jewish mothers, can claim the mantle of Jewishness.

I ignore the number of Jewish kings and princes who, the Bible informs us, married foreign, unkosher daughters for political expediency—such as the devout Jehosaphat who, as a political maneuver against the growing menace of the Arameans and Assyrians, married his son Jehoram to Athaliah, the daughter of Jezebel no less! Consider this passage from Isa. 1:11–18:

> To what purpose is the multitude of your sacrifices unto me? saith the Lord. I am full of the burnt offerings of rams, and the fat of fed beasts; and I delight not in the blood of bullocks, or of lambs or of he-goats. . . . Your hands are full of blood. Wash you, make you clean, put away the evil doings before mine eyes; cease to do evil, learn to do well, seek judgment, relieve the oppressed, judge the fatherless, plead for the widow. Come now and let us reason together.

And this from Martin Buber:

> Rabbi Leib, son of Sarah, used to say about those rabbis who only expound the Torah that: A man should see to it that all his actions are a Torah and that he himself becomes so entirely a Torah that one can learn from his life.

In Buber and Isaiah could be found one of the roots of Judaism: "Let us reason together." It is a Jewish trait to believe in the power of reason, and is both their strength and their downfall. From Isaiah to my mother. Come sit down, have some tea, be calm, talk to me, discuss, say it, be reasonable. I turn to Genesis:

> Lo God created man in his own image, in the image of God created he
> him: male and female created he them.

What a strange concept. *In his own image.* What can it mean? That God is of supreme importance for creating humankind or that humankind is more important because it is created in God's image? From this simple but glorious declaration in Genesis, I believe, stem the two roots of Judaism. Conflicting roots—between those who revere God more than people because He created them, and those who revere people more than God because they were created in His image.

Of the two, the bias of the majority of Jews is toward the rational. Of course in some of us there is the one and a touch of the other, but most modern Jewish writers and intellectuals are the inheritors of the first: that reverence for, and greater preoccupation with, man and his ways rather than with God and the rituals surrounding the glorification of his name. And that inheritance includes the tradition of prophecy, the spirit of tolerance and justice, and the Jewish energy for action; and by prophecy I do not mean futurology, the visionary forecasts of doom-laden or beautiful times to come, which is Messianic prophecy and something quite different; I mean prophecy as criticism, chastisement, warning.

To be Jewish is to be the inheritor of a shared history both of Jewish persecution and of Jewish achievement, and of certain values and ways of perceiving the human situation, *even though not knowing where those values and perceptions are rooted.*

The history of persecution and achievement is written up in books; the values permeate Jewish art, literature, and music and are to do with compassion, tolerance, a sense of justice, a sense of humor and of the absurd, a restless and questioning nature, an international as opposed to a narrow national perspective, a passion for the family, a belief in the sacredness of life on this earth rather than the speculative life hereafter, and a view of charity as godly—toward others and inwardly as self-help in the community. Those values are marked by an absence of the desire for revenge for the persecution of the centuries and by the presence of an instinct to build.

If I am asked "what happens to Jewishness when we take away God as the source of both roots?" I am afraid I would have to quote the central character of my play *Shylock*:

> Imagine this tribe of Semites in the desert. Pagan, wild, but brilliant. A skeptical race, believing only in themselves. Loving but assertive. Full of quarrels and questions. Who could control them? Leader after leader was thrown up, but in a tribe where every father of his family was a leader, who could hold them in check for long? Until one day a son called Abraham was born, and he grew up knowing his brethren very, very well indeed. "I know how to control this arrogant anarchic herd of heathens," he said to himself. And he taught them about one God. Unseen. Of the spirit. That appealed to them, the Hebrews, they had a weakness for concepts of the abstract. An unseen God! Ha! I love it! What an inspiration.

> But that wasn't all. Abraham's real statesmanship, his real stroke of genius was to tell this tribe of exploding minds and vain souls: Behold! An unseen God! God of the universe! of all men! And—"wait for here it comes"—and, of all men you are the chosen ones! Irresistible! In an instant they were quiet. Subdued. "Oh! Oh! Chosen? Really? Us? To do what?" "To bear witness to what is beautiful in creation, and just. A service not a privilege!" "Oh dear! Chosen to bear witness! What an honor! Ssh! Not so loud. Dignity! Abraham is speaking. Respect! Listen to him. Order!" It worked! They had God and Abraham had them. But—they were now cursed. For from that day moved they into a nationhood that had to be better than any other, and, poor things, all nations found them unbearable to live with. What can I do? I'm chosen. I *must* be religious.

If you then ask me what would happen to the Jewish identity if we were to realize that God was created by humankind and that therefore instead of having a relationship between God and humankind we would have a relationship between humankind and its own imaginary projections, I would reply that a relationship between humankind and its own imaginary projections *is merely a succinct description of the evolution of civilization. Someone "imagines" the concept of morality and immediately humanity must work out a relationship with it. The Jew "imagines" God who becomes so central to civilization that people are forced to define themselves alongside him or her.* **This entire volume results from Jews describing their denial of a relationship with an imaginary projection.**

On reflection, after quoting such a passage from my play *Shylock*, I feel I must add one further quality which marks the Jewish spirit: irreverence, a word not to be confused with disrespect. The Jew respects, profoundly, but only that which is earned. In Yiddish there is a special word for it—*koved*. A kind of honoring.

How all these qualities and values were handed down, what paths it took even unto the agnostic or atheist son and daughter is something for which I cannot account. I know only that it traveled through the ages, that it touched many of us, that we drew strength from it, that we warmed more to such dictums as that of Moses Mendelsson that Judaism only judges action and not religious opinion, and that all these things made us feel we could justly lay claim to the identity: *Jew.*

*   *   *

To the reader: Having read my book, please do not hesitate to e-mail your comments, ideas, and suggestions to me at **Exodustohumanism @btinternet.com**—*David Ibry.*

Appendix A

The postcard my father sent from Jerusalem to Mr. A. Finberg (who was the leader of the Hahad Ha-am movement) in London in March 1914 (and answered by Mr. Finberg on April 2), announcing:

> Dear HAHAD HA-AM, Congratulations, Congratulations ("mazal tov")! I will let you into a *secret*: *TODAY* I have purchased for our university a large part (*the highest part*) of a section of the MOUNT OF OLIVES, with a new estate around it. The entire lot from the Englishman, Sir John Gray-Hill. I have invited Dr. Rupin along to sign the deed of sale* ... 250 (dunam) with his house. But keep it a secret! Because we have to buy more and more. Do you know, dear Hahad Ha-am, that the Eng-

---

*In fact my father's name is not mentioned in the deed of sale of the Gray-Hill estate. The explanation of the fact that his name does not appear in the deed of sale lies in the correspondence of 1913 and 1914 between the British Consul in Jerusalem, Mr. McGregor, and the British ambassador in Constantinople, as well as the Foreign Office in London, which correspondence I retrieved from the official British Archives in Richmond. As a result of such correspondence, the British Consul refused to issue my father with a certificate of nationality as required by the Turkish authorities for foreigners to sign deeds of land sales (see Appendix B for a copy of one of those letters).

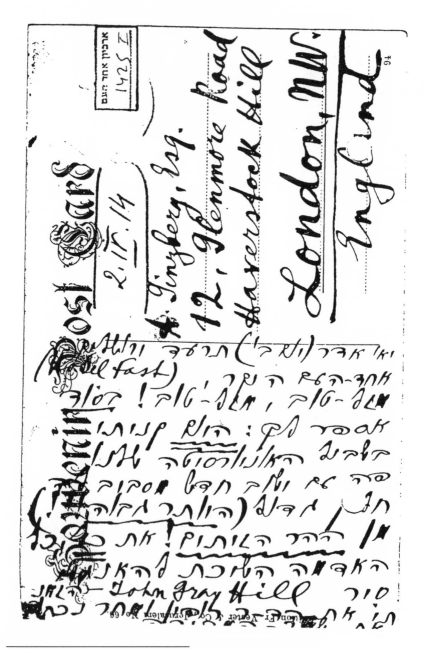

lishman's house is higher (by 8 meters) than the Russian campanile and the German campanile: congratulations!

(The postcard is written in Hebrew and this is my own translation; its original is kept in the Zionist Archives in Jerusalem.)

Whereas Dr. Rupin in his memoirs recalls having been contacted and asked by my father to call on Sir John Gray Hill for the purchase of his house and its estate, in a book recently published by S. Katz and M. Head, *The History of the Hebrew University in Jerusalem—Roots and Beginnings*, there is an article by J. Wartman in which he questions the credibility of my father's claim. His argument is based: (1) on the fact that the above postcard was written two days before the date of the Deed of Sale (obviously the agreement was reached before signing the actual papers) and (2) on my father's writing "in secret" in an open postcard written in Hebrew which even few Jews in Turkish Palestine were familiar with at that time, let alone the Turkish authorities (before Kemal Ataturk).

Mr. Wartman also refers to a book by Hyamson mentioning the correspondence between the British Consul in Jerusalem and the British Ambassador in Constantinople. However, Mr. Wartman does not seem to have examined the actual records of that correspondence and is perhaps not aware of the fact that Hymanson merely offers his own abstract of that correspondence, probably reflecting the abstract at pages 583–84, volume 2 of *The British Consulate in Jerusalem in Relation to the Jews in Palestine (1838–1914)*, published for the Jewish Historical Society of England in 1941.

Now, why is my father's role nowhere acknowledged by the Hebrew University?

Appendix B

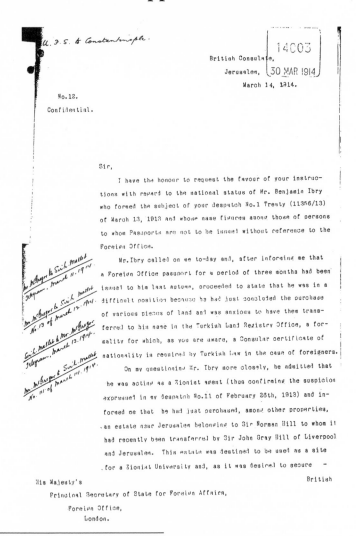

14603

British Consulate,

Jerusalem, 30 MAR 1914

March 14, 1914.

No.12.

Confidential.

Sir,

I have the honour to request the favour of your instructions with regard to the national status of Mr. Benjamin Ibry who formed the subject of your despatch No.1 Treaty (11356/13) of March 13, 1913 and whose name figures among those of persons to whom Passports are not to be issued without reference to the Foreign Office.

Mr. Ibry called on me to-day and, after informing me that a Foreign Office passport for a period of three months had been issued to him last autumn, proceeded to state that he was in a difficult position because he had just concluded the purchase of various pieces of land and was anxious to have them transferred to his name in the Turkish Land Registry Office, a formality for which, as you are aware, a Consular certificate of nationality is required by Turkish Law in the case of foreigners.

On my questioning Mr. Ibry more closely, he admitted that he was acting as a Zionist agent (thus confirming the suspicion expressed in my despatch No.11 of February 26th, 1913) and informed me that he had just purchased, among other properties, an estate near Jerusalem belonging to Sir Norman Hill to whom it had recently been transferred by Sir John Gray Hill of Liverpool and Jerusalem. This estate was destined to be used as a site for a Zionist University and, as it was desired to secure -

His Majesty's

Principal Secretary of State for Foreign Affairs,

Foreign Office,

London.

British

British protection for this institution, the first step towards –
attaining this end was naturally the possession of title-deeds in
the name of a British subject.

I informed Mr.Ibry that, as his passport was no longer valid
I could not grant him a certificate of nationality, but that, if he
would embody his request in a letter to me, I would submit it to
the Foreign Office. He agreed to do so, remarking at the same time
that, as further large purchases were in contemplation, there was
a question of registering them in the name of Lord Rothschild or of
Mr. Claude Montefiore.

As soon as Mr. Ibry brings me his written request I will forward it, but, as the case seems one involving an important principle,
I take advantage of the departure of a mail to place his application
on record, and at the same time I beg to transmit copies of my correspondence with His Majesty's Embassy on the subject of the transaction
in question.

I have the honour to be,

With the highest respect,

Sir,

Your most obedient,

humble servant,

P.J.C.McGregor.